LIES
Young Women
BELIEVE

AND THE TRUTH THAT SETS THEM FREE

STUDY GUIDE

Emily Nguyen

LIES
Young Women
BELIEVE

AND THE TRUTH THAT SETS THEM FREE

STUDY GUIDE

NANCY DeMOSS WOLGEMUTH
AND DANNAH GRESH
WITH ERIN DAVIS

MOODY PUBLISHERS

CHICAGO

Published in association with the literary agency of Wolgemuth & Associates.

Edited by Anne C. Buchanan
Interior design: Julia Ryan / DesignByJulia.com
Cover concept: Amjad Shahzad
Cover design: Erik M. Peterson
Cover photo of apple copyright © 2016 by Dimitrios Stefanidis/iStock (629734762). All rights reserved.
Images: Garden of Eden © Ng/Dreamstime; flourish © Pasko Maksim/Shutterstock; abstract flourish © Gala/Shutterstock

Library of Congress Cataloging-in-Publication Data

Names: Wolgemuth, Nancy DeMoss, author. I Gresh, Dannah, 1967- author.
Title: Lies young women believe and the truth that sets them free : study guide /
   Nancy DeMoss Wolgemuth and Dannah Gresh ; With Erin Davis.
Description: CHICAGO : MOODY PUBLISHERS, 2018.
Identifiers: LCCN 2018006407 (print) I LCCN 2017054230 (ebook) I ISBN
   9780802495129 (ebook) I ISBN 9780802415271
Subjects: LCSH: Teenage girls--Religious life. I Young women--Religious life.
   I Truthfulness and falsehood--Religious aspects--Christianity.
Classification: LCC BV4551.3 (print) I LCC BV4551.3 .D463 2018 (ebook) I DDC
   248.8/33071--dc23
LC record available at https://lccn.loc.gov/2018006407

ISBN: 978-0-8024-1527-1

We hope you enjoy this book from Moody Publishers. Our goal is to provide high-quality, thought-provoking books and products that connect truth to your real needs and challenges. For more information on other books and products written and produced from a biblical perspective, go to www.moodypublishers.com or write to:

Moody Publishers
820 N. LaSalle Boulevard
Chicago, IL 60610

5 7 9 10 8 6 4

Printed in the United States of America

CONTENTS

You'll get even more out of this study
if you find a friend to do it with you. Better yet,
find a group of friends! (In the back of this book,
you'll find some ideas for how to start a group.)
If you're leading a group discussion of
Lies Young Women Believe, look for the
symbol next to questions that would
work well for group discussion.

Getting Started

"You will know the truth, and the truth will set you free."
(JOHN 8:32)

✦ HEY FRIEND!

We're so excited that this book is in your hands. It means you're ready to do some serious work. And that, we believe, is going to lead you to some serious freedom.

We've already rolled up our sleeves and done some of the heavy lifting for you. We developed a plan to uncover lies that you might believe. As part of that plan, we surveyed more than 1000 young women to uncover 25 of the most commonly believed lies in your generation. Then we took that list of lies and set out to uncover God's Truth, praying all along the way that God's Spirit would direct our work.

If you read *Lies Young Women Believe*, you'll get a good glimpse at how you can be free. In essence, we introduced you to Truth in the book.

But being introduced to someone or something isn't the same as *knowing* that person or thing. Jesus said, "You will *know* the truth, and the truth will set you free." We want you to *know* Truth. It's time for you to roll up your sleeves to move past the introductions.

> Most of the Scriptures we quote will be from the English Standard Version of the Bible. Occasionally we'll use the New International Version. When we do, we'll put the handy-dandy "NIV" there so you will know where that verse came from! If you prefer to memorize from a different translation, that's totally okay.

That's where this Study Guide comes in. This book is designed to help you go deeper in understanding and applying the message of *Lies Young Women Believe* (updated version, 2018). You have nine sessions of Bible study, personal application, and discussion suggestions in your hands. Think of this as your private journal as you go through this study. All you need to do is read the chapter or chapters in *Lies Young Women Believe* that correspond to the week of study you're about to begin. Then, keep this book close for daily, thought-provoking assignments that will take you from an introductory look at Truth to a personal, firsthand knowledge of Truth.

Well, what are you waiting for?

LET'S GET STARTED!

✦ Nancy, Dannah, and Erin

The Landscape of Lies

This week, you have a lot of reading to do, including the introduction and chapters 1–3 in *Lies Young Women Believe* (*LYWB* for short!). It gets easier after this week. We'll digest things one chapter at a time, so read a chapter when the assignment appears.

Catching a Glimpse

"Back in the garden, Eve met an imposter with a diabolical agenda. He wanted Eve to become his slave by rejecting God and His purposes for her life. The serpent craftily asked, "Did God actually say, 'You shall not eat of any tree in the garden'?" (Genesis 3:1). That's not exactly what God had said, but it certainly sounded similar. God had told Adam (and Eve) they couldn't eat from the Tree of the Knowledge of Good and Evil. Satan used a clever combination of half-truths and falsehoods *posing* as Truth. ❧ He began by planting doubts in Eve's mind about what God had actually said. . . . He wanted her to turn her back on God, to reject His Truth, and to believe his carefully crafted lies . . . and she did. ❧ And that's exactly what the great Imposter wants you to do."

(*Lies Young Women Believe*, page 20)

KNOW the TRUTH

A critical element of this study will be concentrating your focus on the Truth found in God's Word. We want to encourage you to memorize a Scripture for each week of this study. (You can do it!)

The first verse we want to encourage you to memorize is to the right. We also have these verses on an insert in the back of the book that you can cut out and carry with you.

"So flee youthful passions and pursue righteousness, faith, love, and peace, along with those who call on the Lord from a pure heart."

(2 TIMOTHY 2:22)

DAY ONE:
Blazing Lies

 READ

Read the Introduction: Blazing Lies in *LYWB* (pages 9–15).

 REALIZE

***Realize* means "to make real or actual."** That's what we want to do with this section of each day's study. We want to "make real or actual" the Truth that you've just read. This is where you'll roll up your sleeves and move from just being "introduced" to the Truth in the book to making it so real in your life that you "know" it.

1. Look up 2 Peter 2:19. Rewrite the verse in your own words in the space provided.

----

2. Here are a few of the questions posed in the Introduction to *LYWB*. Record your responses below. (Be honest!)

Are there consuming areas of your life that you can't stop thinking about—perhaps food, guys, or your appearance?

Do you feel as if your life is being controlled by powerful emotions—like fear, depression, anger, loneliness, jealousy, or self-pity?

Are there harmful habits or destructive patterns you can identify in your life—things like cutting yourself, drinking, using drugs, or sexual activity—that you just can't seem to change or let go of?

----

3. Did you take the "what's-the-status-of-your-lying-embers?" quiz? In case you haven't, we've included it here. WHY NOT TAKE IT NOW?

>>> **Circle the word or set of words** that reflect how you feel or respond most of the time. (Select one per pair.)

1 **Relaxed** >>> or Totally stressed-out

2 Happy-to-be-single or **Gotta-have-a-guy**

3 Good-with-what-ya-got or **Ugly**

4 FORGIVEN OR GUILTY

5 Definitely-taking-my-problems-to-God-first or **Gotta-ask-my-friends-for-advice**

6 Got-just-enough-friends or > **LONELY**

7 **Friendly** or > Totally PMS-ing

8 AUTHENTIC **OR** HYPOCRITICAL

9 In-control-of-my-tech-world or Would-**DIE**-without-texting-and-social media

10 Confident-in-my-stand-to-be-pure or **Ashamed-to-stand-alone**

11 Content-with-what-ya-got or **MUST**-shop-now

12 **The-real-deal or Different-depending-on-who-I'm-with**

13 **Walking-in-victory** or Unable-to-overcome-certain-sins

14 Content-to-submit or Angry-at-my-parents

15 **Confident-of-God's-protection** or Afraid-of-Satan

> Look at the words you circled. What might these words reveal about the condition of your emotions and relationships?

4. Remember Erin's story in the introduction of _Lies Young Women Believe_ (pages 9–10) (Fun fact: that is the very same Erin who helped write this Bible study and who runs LiesYoungWomenBelieve.com. Freedom is possible!) Erin was controlled by fear and experienced frequent panic attacks. Her fear was the result of believing lies, but it took her a long time to see that. The biggest lie she believed was "everyone leaves." What Scripture verse would _you_ use to counteract that lie with Truth? Write it down below.

_____

_____

_____

_____

R̲ RESPOND

Respond means to "answer" or to "take action." We want you to do more than just realize the Truth. We want you to act on it! Each day we will guide you through a series of questions or activities designed to help you respond to the Truth you've encountered. This is where it gets personal as you apply Truth directly to your life. If you do this study as part of a group, we'll guide you back to discuss some of these questions together.

1. Often, it's easier to see the lies that others believe, than it is to see how you've been deceived. What are some lies you see the young women around you, especially your friends, believing?

_____

_____

_____

_____

_____

2. How would you like your life to change as a result of this study?

_____

_____

_____

_____

_____

 **PRAY ABOUT IT**

To dig deep, spend time praying about what you're learning in the Word during this study. Ask God to help you see lies and replace them with His Truth. We've included space at the end of each day for you to journal. You can pray silently or out loud, but we'd like to challenge you to record your prayers right here in this book. As you look back, you will be amazed at how God has faithfully responded to you. We'll get you started at the end of each day of study.

Jesus, I want to grow emotionally, spiritually, and relationally as a result of this study. I pray that You will reveal areas of spiritual and emotional bondage in my life and any lies I've believed that are keeping me enslaved. Show me the Truth I need to know to experience freedom, especially in the areas of . . .

DAY TWO:
The Origin of Lies

 READ

Read chapter 1: The Deceiver in *LYWB* (pages 17–23).

 REALIZE

1. Consider today quiz time! Take a stab at the following questions about Satan, and then check your answers by taking a deeper look at a few Scripture passages that tell us about God's archenemy.

>> **A.** If you could describe Satan's physical appearance, based on Scripture, what words would you use?

. . . . big and hairy   . . . . black and scaly

. . . . bright and beautiful   . . . . short and slimy

It might be surprising to realize that Satan would best be described by the words *bright* and *beautiful*! Read 2 Corinthians 11:14 and Ezekiel 28:12.

How can the reality of Satan's appearance affect our tendency to believe his lies?

>> **B.** According to Scripture, what is Satan's native language?

. . . . Latin   . . . . Lying

. . . . Pig Latin   . . . . Jive

Look up John 8:44 to be sure your answer is correct. (Though you probably don't need any help!) What does the writer mean when he writes that lying is Satan's *native* tongue?

>> **C.** Why was Satan cast out of heaven?

. . . . pride   . . . . bad breath

. . . . failure to clean his room   . . . . shining his wings

Of course, Satan wasn't kicked out of heaven for not cleaning his room! Ezekiel 28:12–19 describes Satan's fall. Look it up. What specific character traits led to his downfall?

_____

_____

2. Look up Genesis 2:15–3:10 in your Bible. We want you to thoroughly digest this story. (So much of this book hinges on your understanding of Eve's fall.) As you read the passage, fill in the blanks to review key thoughts.

❖ *"The L*ORD *God took the man and put him in the garden of Eden to work it and keep it. And the L*ORD *God commanded the man, saying, '_____*

_____ . . .'

(Genesis 2:15–17).

❖ *"Now the serpent was more _____ than any other beast of the field that the L*ORD *God had made. He said to the woman, '_____?' And the woman said to the serpent, '_____ but God said,*

'_____.' But the serpent said to the woman,

'_____. For God knows that when you eat of it your eyes will be opened, and you will be like God, knowing good and evil.'

"So when the woman saw that the tree was _____, and that it was a

_____, and that the tree was to be _____, she took

of its fruit and _____, and she also gave some to

_____and he _____. Then the eyes of

both were opened, and they knew that they were naked. And

they sewed fig leaves together and made themselves loincloths.

*"And they heard the sound of the L*ORD *God walking in*

the garden in the cool of the day, and the man and his

_____ among the trees of the garden. But

*the L*ORD *God called to the man and said to him, '_____?'*

And he said, '_____

_____.'" (Genesis 3:1–10).

❖ We're going to do some fill in the blanks on key Bible passages throughout this study. Just like the memory passages, the fill-in-the-blank exercises are based on the English Standard Version. If you don't have an ESV Bible, you can look up these verses online at BibleGateway.com or download a Bible reading app like YouVersion.

3. The story of Adam and Eve in the Garden of Eden is likely a familiar one. Let's look at it closely.

A. Who is the deceiver in these passages? _____

B. What specific lies does he tell to Eve? _____

_____

_____

_____

C. What are the consequences? _____

_____

_____

_____

4. OK, let's take a closer look at how Eve's deception began. Look up Genesis 2:16–17. Fill in the blanks of God's actual command to Adam:

" You may surely eat from _____ tree in the garden; but of the tree of the _____ you shall _____ eat, for in the day that you eat of it you shall _____."

Now look up Genesis 3:1. Fill in the blanks of what Satan said to Eve:

" Did God actually say, 'You shall not eat of _____ tree in the _____"?

Satan began his deception by planting doubts in Eve's mind about what God had *actually* said. God was clear. Adam and Eve had freedom to eat from every tree except one. Satan questioned that freedom by subtly modifying what God had said. The result was Eve and then Adam doing something God had warned would have negative consequences.

We often doubt that a relationship, emotion, or activity is truly harmful *even when God's Word specifically warns against it.*

[lies young women believe]

5. Look up Jeremiah 29:11. How does Satan's desire for our destruction differ from God's desire for our lives?

God desires for us to live abundant lives. He wants you to experience true freedom, joy, peace, and contentment. Our goal in this study is to move you toward His desire for you.

R RESPOND

1. Is there an area of your life where God's Word warns that an activity will cause you harm, but you have chosen to participate anyway? For example, maybe you sometimes expose yourself to "just one" sexual scene in movies here and there (Ephesians 5:3) or you use language that "everyone else is using" but that's negative, unkind, or filthy (Philippians 4:8). What is one area where you are not heeding God's commandments?

----

2. Sin always has consequences, even though we may not experience them right away. What are some consequences Christians may face when they sin, especially as it relates to the sin you wrote about above?

----

3. In what area of your life do you think you may be experiencing consequences for disobeying God?

----

4. If you haven't already done so, find a friend (or a few friends!) who would like to do this study with you. Then, ask someone to pray for you in the area you wrote about above.

PRAY ABOUT IT

Jesus, give me the discernment to recognize the tactics of the Enemy. I am experiencing the consequences of lies I've believed in the area of . . .

DAY THREE:
The Power of Lies

 ## READ

Read chapter 2: The Deceived in *LYWB* (pages 25–31).

 ## REALIZE

💬 **1. Look up Psalm 119:11 and write it in your own words here.**

If we dwell on God's Word, it seems we get a super-ability to overcome sin and walk in Truth. This lets us enjoy the abundant life God desires for us.

💬 **2. Why is it so surprising, then, that the opposite can also be true?** When we dwell on the world's messages and our own fleshly desires, we fall prey to Satan's plan for our destruction. Why do you think it's so hard for us to live as if we really believe this simple Truth?

3. Eve dwelled on Satan's messages and her own desires instead of God's words. The progression looked like this >>>>>>>>>>

It's obvious that she began to *listen* when she heard the serpent's voice. Read Genesis 3:6 below and circle what she began to *dwell* on concerning the tree.

> *"So when the woman saw that the tree was good for food, and that it was a delight to the eyes, and that the tree was to be desired to make one wise, she took of its fruit and ate, and she also gave some to her husband who was with her, and he ate."*

After she dwelled on the lie, she started to *believe* what Satan had told her. Now, underline how she *acted on* her desires.

Eve cooperated with Satan by dwelling on lies rather than the Truth of God's Word.

THE PROGRESSION OF **EVE'S LIE**

Eve listened to a lie.
She got close to the Serpent and entertained his suggestion.

Eve dwelled on the lie.
She conversed with him and considered what he said.

Eve believed the lie.
She believed the Serpent's promise was more trustworthy than what God had said.

Eve acted on the lie.
She ate the fruit.

RESPOND

💬 **1. In chapter 2, we introduced you to a girl we called Caitlyn.** She moved quite quickly from being a wide-eyed, happy twelve-year-old to a bulimic who was fighting for her life. Lots of girls today focus on the world's messages about beauty and value. They often end up fighting battles similar to Caitlyn's. What are some ways the world presents the message that being underweight is healthy? List them on the left side below.

THE SOURCE OF THOSE LIES

(Example: Following models on social media)

LIES I'M BELIEVING

(Example: Beautiful girls are worth more)

First, we listen to the lie. If we dwell on those lies, we begin to believe them. On the right side, write examples of lies we begin to believe about ourselves in the area of beauty and value if we dwell on the world's messages

2. Eve cooperated by dwelling on lies rather than trusting God. We do the same thing. Instead of spending time in God's Word cultivating inner beauty, we spend hours in front of the mirror or at the gym, focused on our physical appearance. Calculate the amount of time you spent last week reading your Bible and praying versus looking in the mirror or working out. Write the number of minutes for each day of the week.

	BIBLE / PRAYER	MIRROR / WORKING OUT
Sunday		
Monday		
Tuesday		
Wednesday		
Thursday		
Friday		
Saturday		

Is this an accurate reflection of how you typically spend your time?

3. We'd like you to set *one* reasonable goal in this area—to help you increase the time you spend reading the Word. Here are some ideas to get you started.

- Commit to spend 15 minutes reading your Bible each day when you get home from school.
- Read a chapter of Proverbs each day for the next month.
- Determine not to look at your phone until after you've spent time reading and meditating on God's Word.

Those are some ideas we thought of, but you know what motivates you better than we do! Spend a few minutes thinking about how you can stay motivated to spend more time dwelling on the Truth. Then, complete this sentence with the commitment you are making:

I commit to spend more time dwelling on the Truth by . . .

_____

_____

_____

PRAY ABOUT IT

Jesus, uncover lies in my life. Expose me to Your powerful Truth. Especially in the area of . . .

The Power of Truth

 ## READ

Read chapter 3: The Truth in *LYWB* (pages 33–37).

 ## REALIZE

1. Fill in the blanks for the following passages.

"Jesus said to him, ' _____ am the _____ , and the _____ ,

and the _____ .'" (JOHN 14:6)

"So Jesus said to the Jews who had believed in him, 'If you _____

in my _____ , you are truly my _____ , and you will

_____ the _____ and the _____ will set you

_____ .'" (JOHN 8:31–32)

"Your _____ is _____ ." (JOHN 17:17)

Based on these verses, write a concise definition of Truth:

> TRUTH IS _____ _____ .

Truth is Jesus Christ. He is the standard or original for Truth. He reveals Truth to us through His written Word.

2. Read John 1:14 and circle the name of Jesus that is presented in that verse.

WONDERFUL COUNSELOR   THE WORD   PRINCE OF PEACE

Jesus is the *living* Word of God. The Bible is the *written* Word of God. Our lives should be in agreement with every word God has given us in the Bible and in Jesus Christ.

3. There is tremendous power in Truth as we find it in the Word of God. Jesus told us about this in John 8:31–32. Look those verses up and write what powerful gift we get when we follow Truth.

_____

_____

4. What did Jesus mean when He said that the Truth had the power to set us free? What does it set us free from?

_____

_____

R↑ RESPOND

1. Not everyone believes in absolute truth. Some believe that "truth" is whatever *you* want it to be. You might hear them say things like "live *your* truth." Describe a situation in your school, society, or the news that illustrates this perspective on "truth."

_____

_____

_____

_____

_____

_____

_____

_____

2. What did Kelly discover was at the heart of her battle with anorexia? How did she find freedom from that bondage?

_____

_____

_____

3. What is one area of your life where you need to be set free? Ask God to help you begin to identify any lies you believe and to help you turn to Christ and His Word to set you free from any deception and bondage you are experiencing. By faith, thank Him that His Truth can set you free!

PRAY ABOUT IT

Jesus, I acknowledge that You are Truth and that You can set me free from every sinful bondage. I need the power of Your Truth in my life. Help me find freedom through the Truth, specifically in the area of . . .

ACT **At the conclusion of each week, we will encourage you to put truth into action.** Some of these steps will be fun. Others will be challenging. All of them are meant to expose the power of lies in your life and to replace those lies with Truth from God's Word.

 These are great activities for you to complete or discuss with others during your small group study!

SATURATE YOUR LIFE WITH TRUTH <<

For the next week, we want you to saturate your life with Truth. Find some Scriptures that are particularly meaningful to you. You can even write those on the blank memory cards in the back of the book. If you don't know where to start, concentrate on verses that spell out God's love for you. (John 3:16 and Psalm 45:11 are examples.) The concordance in the back of your Bible is a great tool to help with this as well. You could also look at the appendix in the back of *Lies Young Women Believe* where we have done some of the research for you and provide truth verses based on various topics.

Write these verses out and cover your world with them. Place a copy on your bathroom mirror, in your car, in your textbooks. (Don't glue them onto your books . . . we wouldn't want you to get in trouble!) Come up with creative ways to remind yourself of these verses throughout the day. **Allow the power of God's Word to begin to loosen the power of lies in your life.**

Lies About God

This week you'll read chapter 4: Lies about God in *LYWB*.

Catching a Glimpse

{ "If you have wrong thinking about God, you will have wrong thinking about everything else. What you believe about God will determine the way you live. If you believe things about Him that aren't true, you will eventually act on those lies and end up in bondage." }

(*Lies Young Women Believe*, page 42)

KNOW the TRUTH

This week, we'd like to see you memorize this passage about how very much God values you!

"Are not five sparrows sold for two pennies? And not one of them is forgotten before God. Why, even the hairs of your head are all numbered. Fear not; you are of more value than many sparrows."

(LUKE 12:6–7)

God Is Not Enough

 READ

Read the beginning of chapter 4 and Lie #1, "God is not enough," in *LYWB* (pages 41–44).

 REALIZE

1. Look up the following passages and jot a brief summary of each in the space provided.

✤ Psalm 37:4 Delight yourself in the Lord, and he will give you the desires of your heart

✤ Psalm 107:8-9 8/ Let them give thanks to the Lord for his unfailing love
9/ for and his wonderful deeds for mankind, for he satisfies the thirsty and fills the hungry with good things

✤ Matthew 5:6 Blessed are those who hunger and thirst for righteousness, for they will be filled.

✤ Philippians 4:19 You can be sure that God will take care of everything you need, his generosity exceeding even yours in the glory of that pours from Jesus

What promise do these passages have in common?

_____

_____

2. The Bible clearly tells us that God is able to handle whatever life throws at us and that He is able to truly satisfy the deepest longings and desires of our hearts. In fact, nothing else can ever truly satisfy us. Even so, almost 90 percent of the young, *Christian* women we surveyed agreed with the statement "God is *not* enough to satisfy." Why do you think that they answered this way?

_____

_____

_____

We might *say* "God is enough for me," but in our hearts we may not really believe that is true. What are some ways young women today might finish this sentence, if they were being completely honest:

"IN ORDER TO BE HAPPY, I NEED GOD *plus* _____."

Example: *parents who understand me*

3. Psalm 23 is chock-full of promises of God's commitment and ability to meet our needs. Fill in key points from this passage in the space provided.

"The Lord is my _____; I shall _____ _____.

He makes me_____ _____ in _____ _____.

He _____ _____ beside still waters.

He _____ my _____.

He _____ _____ in paths of _____ for his name's sake.

"Even though I walk through the valley of the shadow of death,

I _____ _____ _____ _____,

for you are _____ _____; your rod and your staff,

they _____ me.

"You prepare a table before me in the presence of my enemies;

you _____ my _____ with oil; my cup overflows.

Surely _____ and _____ shall follow me all the days of my life,

and I shall _____ in the _____ of the _____ forever."

R RESPOND

1. OK, let's bring this familiar Psalm home and personalize it for your life! Use the left column to make a list of how the psalmist expresses God's character and His promises. Use the right column to write a practical explanation of what that means for us. We've given you an example to get you started.

GOD'S CHARACTER AND PROMISES ⟶ WHAT THAT MEANS TO ME TODAY

He is my Shepherd!   If I follow Him, I'll end up in the right place!

_____   _____

_____   _____

_____   _____

_____   _____

_____   _____

_____   _____

_____   _____

_____   _____

_____   _____

_____   _____

_____   _____

_____   _____

2. Let's look at whether you are truly looking to God to be your everything. To do that, you'll answer two questions: "What possessions, activities, or relationships are most important to me?" And, "How would it affect my life if these were taken away?" Use the prompts below to guide your thinking.

I can't imagine living without _____ because _____.

If my relationship with _____ ended, I would feel _____.

If I couldn't participate in _____ anymore, I would be _____.

3. Anything or anyone other than God that we feel we can't live without or that means more to us than God, can become an idol in our lives. Based on what you wrote above, can you identify any idols in your life?

_____

_____

🅟 PRAY ABOUT IT

Jesus, thank You for promising to meet my needs. I want to learn to be deeply and fully satisfied with You. I confess that I have been looking to things and people other than You to satisfy my heart—things like:

_____

_____

_____

_____

_____

_____

God Is Not Really Involved in My Life

 READ

Read Lie #2, "God is not really involved in my life," in *LYWB* (pages 44–46).

 **REALIZE**

1. It's quiz time again! This time, let's test your knowledge of world events. (Groan!) We promise these questions won't be too tough.

A. Who was the first president of the United States of America?

a . . . . Curious George   c . . . . George Strait

(b) . . . George Washington   d . . . . George Clooney

B. A pharaoh is an ancient ruler of which country?

a . . . . Spain   c . . . . Portugal

(b) . . . Egypt   d . . . . Jamaica

C. Who did God command to build an ark and stock it full of every kind of animal?

a . . . . Mickey   c . . . . Minnie

(b) . . . Noah   d . . . . Daffy

How'd you do? We knew you'd figure out that the answer to all three questions was b. (You're smart!) But what was the point of those silly questions? We simply wanted to remind you that the world is a big place with lots going on. Is it possible that the God who manages world affairs knows and cares about the details of our lives? This is where many in your generation seem to get hung up. One girl from our focus groups summed it up this way.

> *"God is so big. He has so much to take care of with wars and natural disasters and stuff like that. I find it hard to believe that He cares about what is going on in my life."*

It *is* hard to believe, isn't it? We can hardly imagine that the God of the universe, the same God who created and sustains all life, could care about the details of our circumstances. Because this truth is so difficult to wrap our minds around, many young women have drawn the false conclusion that God is not personally involved in their lives. This is contrary to the Word of God.

2. Look up the following verses and write them out in the space provided.

✦ Isaiah 65:24 _"And it shall come to pass, that b4 they call, I will answer; and while they are yet speaking, I will hear"._

✦ Luke 12:6–7 _6. Are not 5 sparrows sold for two pennies? Yet not one of them is forgotten by God. 7, You are worth more than many sparrows even every hair of your head._

✦ 1 Peter 5:7 _Cast all your anxiety on him bc he cares for you._

3. Returning to the verses you just wrote above, underline words or phrases that indicate that God cares about your circumstances.

4. Write your memory verse for this week below. It's a great reminder that God is specifically concerned with you!

R RESPOND

1. Dannah told a story in *LYWB* of God's amazing provision in Africa when her husband had a bloody nose. Can you think of a story like that from your own life? Write about a situation where God intervened in your life and provided what you needed or asked for.

_____
_____
_____
_____
_____
_____
_____

2. Can you think of a time when you asked God for something and He didn't give you what you wanted, but in the long run you saw that He did what was best for you? Write about that experience below.

Probably the consistency I gained through time.
I was always procastinated whenever I did sth and even
hade little interest in doing the things I like. I asked
if he could help w/ it but no, he didn't. Still, after
some time, when I'm more mature, I realized now know
that God had helped me realized the problem was me,
not anyone else and I had overcome it

3. What are two or three fears or concerns you are currently struggling with?

- The fear of failing when I studied hard.
- Health (?) Sleeplessness

[lies young women believe]

God knows everyone, know ~~their~~ our doings
→ He cares

4. Read Psalm 139:1–6, 17. What do these verses tell you about God? How does the Truth of this passage apply to your life and the issues you are facing? → *Find ease with God by my side and face challenges ~~certain~~ firmly but calmly.*

❤ PRAY ABOUT IT

Father, thank You for caring about my circumstances and for being involved in my life. I cannot always feel Your presence, but I know that You are always with me and that You care about these specific situations I am dealing with:

Academic performances at school

Get into a good college, know my major
↳ determined

Spread benevolence to everyone   (has to)

Know where I'm heading / aiming at

Have to be a good sis / daughter / person in my society
Guide me to

Get through
+
I (OVER) IT

DAY THREE:
God Should Fix My Problems

 READ

Read Lie #3, "God should fix my problems," in *LYWB* (pages 46–49).

REALIZE

1. Fill in the blanks for the following passages.

❖ "Count it all ___joy___, my brothers, when you meet ___trials___ of various kinds, for you know that the testing of your faith produces ___steadfastness___. And let ___steadfastness___ have its ___full effect___, that you may be ___perfect___ and ___complete___, lacking in ___nothing___." (JAMES 1:2–4)

❖ "Not only that, but we ___rejoice___ in our ___sufferings___, knowing that suffering produces ___endurance___, and endurance produces ___character___, and character produces ___hope___." (ROMANS 5:3–4)

According to these passages, what are the results of trials?

They help us in "changing" ourselves in a good way, forming a hope and keeping the optimism, the hope then one day we'll reach it.
→ Closer to God

2. What is your reaction to the statement that we wrote in *LYWB*: "God is more concerned with changing us and glorifying Himself than about solving all our immediate problems" (page 47)?

He assists us spiritually, so there's nothing wrong about God &t does not solve our immediate problems. Moreover it is us who eventually change, so focus on ourselves first then use God's assistance in helping u change.

[lies young women believe]

3. God cares about your circumstances and He wants you to talk to Him about your problems. But a balanced prayer life includes more than petitions for our own needs. Read the following Scriptures and write down other things we should include in our time with God.

Psalm 136:1 _Give thanks unto the Lord; for he is good: for his mercy endureth forever_

Psalm 32:5

James 5:16

Psalm 46:10

1. Does your prayer life reflect that you believe this lie on some level? If so, how?

2. Can you think of an example from your own life where Christ used a difficult circumstance to develop growth in you? Write about that experience in the space provided.

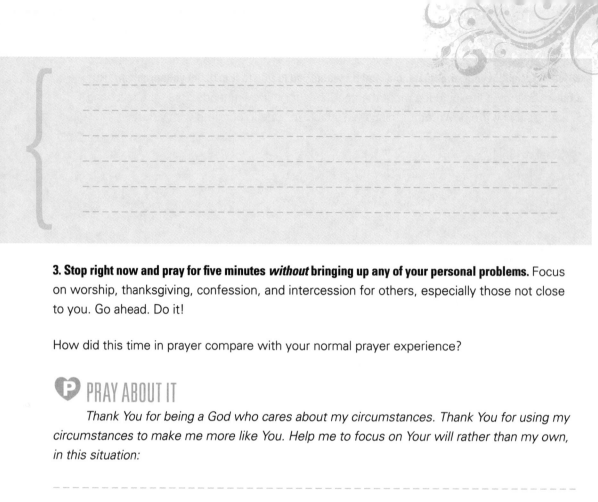

3. Stop right now and pray for five minutes *without* bringing up any of your personal problems. Focus on worship, thanksgiving, confession, and intercession for others, especially those not close to you. Go ahead. Do it!

How did this time in prayer compare with your normal prayer experience?

P PRAY ABOUT IT

Thank You for being a God who cares about my circumstances. Thank You for using my circumstances to make me more like You. Help me to focus on Your will rather than my own, in this situation:

[lies young women believe]

DAY FOUR:
God Is Just Like My Father

 ## READ

Read Lie #4, "God is just like my father," in *LYWB* (pages 49–51).

REALIZE

1. How does Scripture describe our heavenly Father? Let's dig into the Word and find out. Look up the verses listed below and then write down the characteristics of God that each one points out.

James 1:17 _____

_____

1 John 3:1 _____

_____

Matthew 7:9–11 _____

_____

Hebrews 12:7–10 _____

_____

2. In this chapter we pointed out that God is a Father, but He is not like any man you've ever known. Which of the qualities highlighted in the Scriptures listed above are supernatural (i.e., not found in humans)?

_____

_____

_____

_____

_____

3. Let's take a closer look at one of the quotes from this chapter.

"My relationship with my dad hasn't been so good for the past few years. I used to be 'his girl,' but now he's distant and I don't know what I've done wrong. I cannot relate to God the way I relate to my dad, or we wouldn't relate at all." (p. 49)

What counsel would you offer this girl based on what you've read in this chapter and in the Word?

 # RESPOND

1. Go back to the list of characteristics you outlined in question one of "realize" on page 39. Place a star beside the characteristics of God that remind you of your earthly dad. Circle the characteristics of God that are not like your human father. Is your perception of your dad largely positive or negative?

2. OK, let's try something that may be difficult, but could be really helpful! Write a letter to your dad explaining how your relationship with him has affected your spiritual walk. If his influence has been largely positive, tell him so. If it has been largely negative, ask God to show you something about your dad you can be grateful for. Then if you feel the freedom, gently share how God has used even the difficult things in your relationship. Be respectful. This is not an open invitation to trash your father. You can write your letter right here:

DEAR DAD!

[lies young women believe]

If your dad is active in your life, we'd encourage you to give him the letter once you're finished. Use it as a tool to open the lines of communication. If your dad is not active in your life or you feel he would not respond well to what you have written, read the letter to a friend, youth pastor, or mentor. Together, talk through how your relationship with your father has impacted how you relate to God.

ⓟ PRAY ABOUT IT

Dear God, thank You for being a father like no other. Help me better understand Your role as my heavenly Father. Especially, help me understand Your promise to . . .

> **We're assuming you have become a child of God by placing your faith in Jesus Christ. If you don't know whether you are a member of God's family, look ahead to page 61 where we explore the topic!**

A ACT Become a _LYWB_ roving reporter! Have you believed lies about God? You are not alone. To explore this area further, we want you to grab your phone and start filming. Interview your family, your friends, and your classmates and find out who they think God is. Consider yourself our newest _LYWB_ roving reporter. Go out there and get the scoop on what the people around you believe about God. We bet you'll uncover a lie or two. You can even post your videos to Instagram or YouTube with the hashtags #LiesYoungWomenBelieve and #LYWBblog so we can take a peek. Who knows, we may even use one in a future blog post!

Lies About Satan and Lies About Myself

This week, you'll read chapter 5: Lies about Satan (pages 57–67) and chapter 6: Lies about Myself (pages 71–83) in *LYWB*.

Catching a Glimpse

{ "The Bible describes Satan as our adversary, our accuser, our tempter, and the deceiver. He is described as 'a roaring lion, seeking someone to devour' (1 Peter 5:8). Even though he is limited, with God's permission, Satan can and often does make life difficult for us." }

(*Lies Young Women Believe*, page 59)

KNOW the TRUTH

This week, use your memorization muscle to this passage about God's strength. We love to consider these verses when we are feeling particularly vulnerable to the enemy.

"Finally, be strong in the Lord and in the strength of his might. Put on the whole armor of God, that you may be able to stand against the schemes of the devil. For we do not wrestle against flesh and blood, but against the rulers, against the authorities, against the cosmic powers over this present darkness, against the spiritual forces of evil in the heavenly places."

(EPHESIANS 6:10–12)

Everything Bad That Happens Is Spiritual Warfare

 READ

Before you tackle your reading assignment for the week, skip ahead to the Realize section and answer question number one. We want you to have a fresh, untouched perspective to answer this question!

REALIZE

1. Write your definition of "spiritual warfare."
spiritual warfare—or enemies—that we'll face.

be involved in / facing _b_

e.g. insecurities of our body
but we keep eating —> m
_OR v_

fight our own thoughts
urself is ur greatest
enemy

Now, let's examine your definition to see if it hold
Read the introduction to chapter 5 and Lie #5, "Ev
warfare," in *LYWB* (beginning on page 57).

2. We're in a battle, but just what are we battling? Too often, we think that if we're facing discouragement, Satan must certainly be in the picture. But is he? Use the verses listed below to answer the following true or false questions.

❖ **True or False?** Satan is all-knowing just like God. (MATTHEW 24:36)

❖ **True or False?** Satan has unlimited power. (LUKE 22:31–32; JAMES 4:7; EPHESIANS 6:16)

❖ **True or False?** Satan can act without permission from God. (JOB 1:12; 2:6; MATTHEW 4:1–11)

❖ **True or False?** Satan is actively seeking to cause harm to those who believe in God.
(1 PETER 5:8)

❖ **True or False?** Satan is present everywhere at once. (JOB 1:7)

It is true that Satan is always actively seeking to cause harm to those who believe in God. But that doesn't mean he has his eye on you all the time. The rest of the answers are false. Satan doesn't know everything God knows. His power is limited. He cannot do anything without permission from God and he cannot be everywhere at once. So, if our battle is hard and never stops then there must be other enemies to fight.

3. There are two other enemies at work and we addressed them in *LYWB*. Look up the verses below and write at the top of each list the enemy that is mentioned in that group of verses.

>>>

THE ___*flesh*___ ___*blood*___   THE ___WORLD___

Romans 7:25 *God's law*   John 15:18–19
Galatians 5:16 *Spirit*   1 Corinthians 1:18–24
1 Peter 2:11 *desire*

The devil is not lurking under every problem you face. <u>*You* might be the problem.</u> For example, if you feast on chips and soda nonstop, you may end up with health problems. If you give in to sinful, fleshly desires, you will end up in spiritual bondage. Or you may simply be facing the challenge of living in a *fallen world*. For example, if you surf the Internet unfiltered, you may end up seeing porn.

Bottom line: You can't immediately cry "spiritual warfare," assuming that *Satan* has personally attacked you every time you have a problem. You need to take personal responsibility if you've been feeding your flesh or not controlling your exposure to sinful things of this world.

4. Yes, we always face warfare, but we don't always face *Satan* or his demons. Using what you've just studied, fill in the blanks to come up with a more complete definition of "spiritual warfare."

stand FIRM, never back down

"Spiritual warfare" is the daily battle I face to live righteously.

It may include battling the ___Satan___ and his demons, *(flesh)*

but more often it includes the battle to control my own ___*desire / urge*___

and the exposure I allow to the fallen ___world___ in which we live.

R RESPOND

1. Some problems we face are a result of fueling our sinful flesh. Can you write about a time when you faced consequences for feeding your fleshly desires?

Bad grades b/c I had an addiction to game when Covid went out. I couldn't concentrate on studying and always multitasking. Thus, my health did deteriorate for a time, and now I have suppress, control that hook → I FELT BETTER

2. Write about a time when you experienced the sin of this fallen world and realized you needed to build a stronger wall between you and the world.

Bad comments
I ignore these

3. **Let's pause for a heart check!** Think back over the past week.

❧ What choices have you made that have fed sinful behaviors and tendencies?

❧ Have you stuck with the commitment you made on page 21 to spend more time dwelling on Truth this week?

❧ What steps have you been taking to develop a love relationship with God?

These are the kinds of spiritual exercises that will help guard your heart from giving in to the sinful tendencies of your flesh.

[lies young women believe]

Take a few moments to write out your response to any of the questions above or to evaluate the current condition of your heart toward the Lord.

🅟 PRAY ABOUT IT

Jesus, give me discernment in the area of spiritual warfare. Help me recognize when my circumstances are a result of my own actions, the world around me, or the attacks of Satan. I know I need to guard my heart and my relationship with You by . . .

Praying each night, createng a bond with
you, my Lord. Amen

I've Never Been Exposed to Satanic Activities

 READ

Read Lie #6, "I've never been exposed to s

REALIZE

Handwritten note: interprets omens, or a sorcerer, or who cast a spell, call up the dead. → Detestable to the Lord.

1. You already know that you should avoid that mean? Let's take a look at what the Bible has to say on the subject. Look up the following verses and write down the things in each of them God tells us to avoid.

❖ Deuteronomy 18:10–12 _There shall not be found among you anyone who makes his or his daughter pass through the fire, divination, witch_

❖ Leviticus 20:6 _If a person turn to mediums and necromancers, whoring after them, I will set my face against that person and will cut_

❖ Galatians 5:19–21 _works of flesh are evident: sexual immortality, from impurity, sensuality, idolatry, emity, envy, drunkness, and things like these._

DON'T JUDGE PPL

2. In *LYWB*, we reported that 72 percent of youth group participants have read their horoscopes. A lot of the girls we interviewed admitted to watching psychic TV. One group of Christian girls attempted to have a séance, just for fun.

How about you? If you haven't already answered them, here are some questions we presented in *LYWB*. Check it out. Circle yes or no.

"**HAVE YOU EVER** looked at or read your horoscope?" **yes no**

"**HAVE YOU EVER** participated in psychic activities?" **yes no**

"**HAVE YOU EVER** had your palm read?" **yes no**

"**HAVE YOU EVER** played a video game or watched a movie that portrayed demonic forces or witchcraft in a positive way?" **yes no**

3. Read Galatians 5:19–21. Then answer this question: "Do you think that participating in the practices listed above could have a harmful effect on your walk with God?" Why or why not? Be prepared to defend your answer.

[lies young women believe]

4. It's not just séances and palm reading that open the door for Satan to have access in our lives. Certain heart attitudes can be just as dangerous. Beside each of the verses below, write the attitude that can give access to the enemy.

❖ Ephesians 4:26–27 __ Angry ; do not give a foothold to the devil __

❖ 2 Corinthians 2:10–11 __ anyone who forgive, I forgive → Merciful __

❖ 1 Samuel 15:23 __ Rebellion _____

R RESPOND

1. Take this short attitude assessment to see if there are specific areas of your life that are making you vulnerable to Satan's influence.

HOW OFTEN are you angered to the point that you yell, curse, or throw things?
[X] never [ ] rarely [ ] sometimes [ ] often

HOW OFTEN do you imagine yourself "chewing others out" or confronting them over something you are mad about?
[X] never [ ] rarely [ ] sometimes [ ] often

HOW OFTEN do you find yourself in verbal fights with others?
[ ] never [X] rarely [ ] sometimes [ ] often

HOW OFTEN do you find yourself rolling your eyes or arguing when your parents ask you to do something you don't want to?
[ ] never [X] rarely [ ] sometimes [ ] often

HOW OFTEN do you get in trouble at school for disrespecting teachers or administrators?
[X] never [ ] rarely [ ] sometimes [ ] often

HOW OFTEN do you hold resentment in your heart toward someone who has hurt you?
[X] never [ ] rarely [ ] sometimes [ ] often

LOOK CLOSELY AT YOUR ANSWERS. Do they reveal a pattern of anger or rebellion?
Do your answers point to an area of bitterness in your heart?

2. Chances are that you've identified one or more areas where you don't have the right attitude or actions. Confess each of those areas to the Lord. Ask for His forgiveness and grace to overcome that sinful tendency. Then, confess it to a parent, godly friend, or older Christian. Ask them to help hold you accountable and to let you know when they see evidence of this sin recurring in your life.

I used to be harsh and stubborn to my parents, esp my mom. We're the closest but I took it out on her and my siblings. I've found peace — my anger

3. Read Ephesians 6:10–18. What provision has God made for us in the battle against Satan and his evil forces?

Be strong, put on the full armor
Stand firm
Belt of truth: open my eyes to see ur truth and live according to it daily
Breastplate of righteousness: live a holy life
Shoes of the gospel g peace : speak out
Shield of faith, helmet of salvation, sword gspirit

Write down any practical ways you can think of to put on the armor of God this week. Aren't you glad you have this armor?!

Areas of ur life implicated w/ satanic activities
Thank him

ⓟ PRAY ABOUT IT

Take the time to write a longer prayer today. Write a letter to God specifically addressing these things:

- ❧ Ask Him to point out any areas of your life where you are *unknowingly* exposing yourself to satanic activities.

- ❧ Confess areas where you have knowingly exposed yourself to satanic activities.

- ❧ Confess specific attitudes that open your life up to Satan's influence.

- ❧ Ask for discernment to help recognize Satan's influence in the future.

- ❧ Thank Christ for His protection from Satan and His promise to ultimately defeat our Enemy.

Beautiful Girls are Worth More

 READ

Read Lie #7, "Beautiful girls are worth more," in *LYWB* (pages 72–77).

 **REALIZE**

1. It's time to pull out those pencils, crayons, and markers and maybe even a sticker or two. Let's do an art project! Don't worry; you won't be graded on your artistic ability. Your task is fairly simple. Today we're going to explore the subject of beauty.

Rather than describing the so-called perfect woman, we want you to draw her. By the world's standards and in your opinion, what should her size and shape be? How should she style her hair? What should she be wearing? We've given you plenty of space on the next page to be expressive. >

2. Now let's take a look at what the Bible says about beauty. Read the following verses and then fill in the blanks of these Truth statements.

"Charm is deceitful and beauty is vain." (Proverbs 31:30)

Physical beauty is _____*real*_____.

(The word "vain" means empty, worthless, or fleeting.)

"Do not let your adorning be external—the braiding of hair and the putting on of gold jewelry, or the clothing you wear—but let your adorning be the hidden person of the heart with the imperishable beauty of a gentle and quiet spirit, which in God's sight is very precious." (1 PETER 3:3–4)

The beauty that matters most is _____*personality*_____.

"I also want the women to dress modestly, with decency and propriety, adorning themselves, not with elaborate hairstyles or gold or pearls or expensive clothes, but with good deeds, appropriate for women who profess to worship God."
(1 TIMOTHY 2:9–10 NIV)

Inner beauty is revealed by how you _____*treat others*_____.

DRAW THE PERFECT WOMAN HERE.

> > > > >

models ☺

3. We hope you didn't put your crayons or markers away too soon. It's time to draw a beautiful woman again. This time, draw your interpretation of the beauty described in God's Word. Since the Bible tends to focus most on inner beauty, think of a creative way to illustrate what this type of beauty looks like.

> > > > > | IT'S TIME TO DRAW A BEAUTIFUL WOMAN AGAIN.

my sibling and I

me

my brother sister

Ignore
Neglect these
bad
comments

You'll never be
good enough
for this house

thinks of
others
up 3 children

lovely

She's hard
- working

Divorce !!!

best mom I'd wish for

our mom
(simulation
only!)

grateful

[lies young women believe]

 **RESPOND**

💬 **1. In this chapter of *LYWB*, we shared about our own frustrations with beauty.**
(Remember how Nancy talked about her braces and Dannah put on her makeup in the dark?) If we were going to include your beauty story in this chapter, what would it say? Write down an honest peek into your fears and insecurities concerning your appearance.

I was bodyshamed by people I don't know and unfortunately, my relatives also criticize of how I look or specifically my weight. I tried losing 22 pounds but my nainty made me gained the exact weight @ the beginning. Since that day, I started to stop harsh/pushing mysely into hard exercises @ the gym and strict diet, I learned to love this body and treat it w/ grace.

2. Go through your room and your social media pages. Look for anything that could be contributing to the unhealthy belief that beautiful girls are worth more. Check out your walls. Make sure you haven't lined them with images of models, photos that portray individuals who are unrealistically beautiful, or pictures that have likely been airbrushed or altered. Now, consider those you follow on social media. Do they send you images that reflect realistic and wholesome physical beauty, or do they tempt you to over-filter yourself or present yourself in a way that's not godly?

If you've surrounded yourself with messages that could contribute to dwelling on lies this area, get rid of them! What you believe about beauty will be determined by where you look. Remove anything that tempts you to believe that you are anything less than fearfully and wonderfully made by God. Write a list of what you had to get rid of here.

ⓟ PRAY ABOUT IT

Father, help me recognize that I have been "wonderfully made" by You (Psalm 139:14).
I now recognize that I have believed messages about beauty and my physical appearance that
aren't true. Especially . . .

Father, I learned to ignore those bad comments on
my appearance, esp my weight and styles. That's
just how my personality portraits and You, dear
God, shaped and granted me me today. Thank
you and I shall cherish Your creation which is myself.
Amen!

DAY FOUR:
I Have to Perform to Be Loved and Accepted

R READ:

Read Lie #8, "I have to perform to be loved and accepted," in *LYWB* (pages 77–81).

R REALIZE

1. Ninety percent of the girls we surveyed for *LYWB* said they are or have been plagued by the lie that they have to perform to be loved or accepted. Whoa! Let's tackle this one big time. Let's start with the terms "grace" and "works." Write what you think the definition is for each of these words:

❧ "Grace" is ____ *blessings* _____

❧ "Works" is ____ *endeavors* _____

God's "grace" is a free gift. It is God doing good for us when we deserve just the opposite. The love of Christ and the forgiveness of our sins are both expressions of His grace. We can't earn God's grace, and we don't deserve it.

"Works" is a word the Bible uses to describe the "good" things we do to try to be accepted by God. As Christians, we are commanded to do "good works" to express our love and gratitude for what God has done in our lives. But those "good works" do not make us Christians. We could never do enough "works" to earn His gift of forgiveness. That is only a result of His grace and love.

2. What does the Bible say about Christ's love for us? Let's take a look. Fill in the blanks for the following verses.

❧ *"Blessed be the God and Father of our Lord Jesus Christ, who has blessed us in Christ with every spiritual blessing in the heavenly places, even as* ___ *he chose* ~~spiritual blessin~~ us *in him* ___ *before* ___ *the* ___ *creation* ___ *of the* ___ *world*, *that we should be holy and blameless before him. In* ___ *love* *he predestined us for* ___ *adoption* *to himself as sons through Jesus Christ, according to the purpose of his will."* (Ephesians 1:3–5)

According to these verses, when did God's love for us begin? ___ *before the creation of the world*

3. God's Word states that He loved us _before_ we could love Him back. This is a difficult concept for us to grasp, but it is true! God's love was given to you as a result of grace, not as a result of works. That means you can't earn it.

Check out these verses. Rewrite them in your own words in the space provided. (By the way, this can be a useful tool in studying the Bible—it's called "paraphrasing." It can help you meditate on what the verse says and what it means.)

❖ Ephesians 2:8–9 _Work to earn God's gift - grace._

❖ Romans 11:6 _And if by grace, then it cannot be based on works; if it were, grace would no longer be grace_

💬 **4. In _LYWB_, we told you about Sophia.** She was consumed with swimming. It became what she perceived to be her value. What advice would you have given her when she was consumed with swimming?

If you Never let any single loss get to your head. People always makes mistakes, keep building the belief you have and don't be discouraged if you lose.

R RESPOND

💬 **1. Why is it difficult to accept that God's love for you is not based on what you can accomplish or on your ability to be good?**

He created us. God is perfect in any way; howereve imperfect we are, He still loves us.

💬 **2. In what areas do you feel pressure to perform in order to win the favor of God or others?**

Being perfect (?)
perfectionist, always be/do right

Finding God's Free Gift of Salvation

Maybe you have always secretly wondered what it really means to "trust in Christ" or "ask Jesus into your heart." Maybe you've heard of "the gospel" but aren't really sure exactly what that is. Just so we're all on the same page, let's pause and clear things up.

"The gospel" is a term used to describe the good news that Jesus made a way to redeem us from our sin and reconcile us to the Father. Four key biblical teachings are an important part of that good news:

1. God is holy and commands us to be holy, too. Leviticus 19:2 says, "You shall be holy, for I the LORD your God am holy." God is absolutely, completely perfect in every aspect of His nature and His actions—and He requires the same from us.

2. Yet, we are sinful. Romans 3:23 says, "For all have sinned and fall short of the glory of God." In fact, Psalm 51:5 says that we've been sinners since the womb! We were all born with a sinful nature. Our sin keeps us from being able to have a relationship with a holy God. We could never be good enough on our own to earn God's acceptance.

3. Jesus is the only answer to our sin problem. Jesus said, "I am the way, and the truth, and the life. No one comes to the Father except through me" (John 14:6). Jesus is the *only* way to obtain eternal life, but eternal life is not all He makes possible. The Bible says, "For our sake he [God] made him [Jesus] to be sin who knew no sin, so that in him we might become the righteousness of God" (2 Corinthians 5:21). Through Jesus' death on the cross and His resurrection, God provided a way for us to be made holy. (See point #1).

4. God calls us to repent—or turn away from sin and toward godly living— and trust Jesus. Jesus said, "I have not come to call the righteous but sinners to repentance" (Luke 5:32). Since we've already established that we are all sinners, this is very good news! Acts 3:19 says, "Repent therefore, and turn back, that your sins may be blotted out." To repent means to turn away from sin and toward Jesus. This means you stop living for yourself and start living for Jesus. When you trust in Him, He forgives you and gives you His righteousness so that when God looks at you, He sees Jesus' holiness instead of your sin. This is all by God's grace and it is available to anyone who will call out to Jesus in repentance and faith.

If you have never accepted the free gift of God's grace, why not do so right now? Here's how.

Step 1: Admit that you're a sinner and fall short of God's standard of holiness. (Leviticus 19:2; Psalm 51:5; Romans 3:23)

Step 2: Acknowledge that you cannot do anything to save yourself and that Jesus is your only hope. (Isaiah 65:6; John 14:6; 2 Corinthians 5:21)

Step 3: By faith, express to God your desire to repent of your sin and to accept the free gift of salvation that He offers through Christ. (Romans 10:9–10; Ephesians 2:8–9)

Tell someone about it. Sharing your decision with others is an important step to help you grow in your faith. So be sure to tell your parents or your youth pastor or a friend that you've accepted God's free gift of salvation. We'd also love to hear about it. You can tell us on our blog at **LiesYoungWomenBelieve.com.**

◉ PRAY ABOUT IT

Jesus, thank You for the free gift of Your love. Even though I know that Your love for me isn't based on my ability to perform, I still feel pressure to achieve perfection in the area of . . .

study, life and work. I want to be

A▸ACT **For your action step this week, let's tackle one area where you are fueling lies in your thinking.** If it is the television or laptop in your bedroom that allows you to watch shows that are unholy, take it out. Don't just put it somewhere where you can easily retrieve it the next time you're bored. Move it into the family room where you can model accountability. If there is some other item that is tripping you up, get rid of it! Have a yard sale. Donate it to Goodwill.

If it's performance that makes you feel value, take a weeklong fast from the activity you get your sense of worth from. Be willing to take radical steps if needed. Get a note from your parents to take a week off from piano lessons or give your basketball shoes to your pastor's wife for safekeeping. Do what you have to do to stop being consumed by performance.

> We'd love to hear about the actions you've taken and the difference they've made. **Drop by and tell us about it at LiesYoungWomenBelieve.com.** Or follow @LiesYoungWomenBelieve on Instagram or @LYWBblog on Twitter.

Lies About Sexuality

This week, you'll read chapter 7: Lies about Sexuality in *LYWB* (pages 87–103).

Catching a Glimpse

{ "We believe that the lies girls believe about guys, sexuality, and sex are some of the most powerful lies and have the potential to expose girls' hearts to deep, long-term hurt." }

(*Lies Young Women Believe*, p. 87)

KNOW the TRUTH

Here's the verse we'd like you to memorize this week:

"But among you there must not be even a hint of sexual immorality, or of any kind of impurity, or of greed, because these are improper for God's holy people."

(EPHESIANS 5:3 NIV)

It's OK to Date Whoever I Feel Like Dating

R READ

Read the Introduction to Lie #9, "It's OK to date whoever I feel like dating" in chapter 7 of _LYWB_ (pages 87–91).

R REALIZE

1. Read 2 Corinthians 6:14–18. Write this passage in your own words in the space provided.

Do not be yoked / involved (build a relationship w/ unbeliever
God's words: "I will live with them
                and walk among them,
                and I will be their God"
                    and they will be my people".

❖ What do you think it means to be "yoked"?

connected

❖ Grab a dictionary or use an online tool to look up the definition for yoked. Write what you find below.

8th that connects two things or people, usually in a way that unfairly limits freedom.

💬 **2. According to the passage you read in 2 Corinthians, why should we avoid being yoked with someone who is not a Christian?**

Different opinion → Argument
And they won't able to help us when we're
in need and vice versa, still, that will be a hindrance
to us when we're fully committed to God.

💬 **3. Imagine being tied together to someone who is traveling in a different direction than you are.** List several areas where you might have to "travel" in a different direction than your husband if you were to marry a man who is not a believer.

1. Example: sharing your Christian faith with your children

2. _Can't talk anything about God when their presence's there_

3.

4.

5.

R RESPOND

💬 **1. Do you know someone who loves Jesus but is married to a non-Christian?** What challenges have you witnessed in their life or marriage?

Division in thinking
Isolation like distinct

💬 **2. Make a list of reasons why it is unwise to date a non-Christian.**

Can't do anything relating to God together
_   reading bible, praying together_
Arguments likely to happen

3. If you've not already done so, we want to encourage you to take our relationship challenge to date only Christians who share your beliefs and are able to challenge you spiritually. You can view the challenge on **page 91** in *LYWB*.

PRAY ABOUT IT

Today, instead of writing a prayer to God, we want you to make a list of the qualities you most desire in a husband. Feel free to include physical features and personality traits. But spend the most time thinking about what is important to you spiritually. At the top of your list should be the fact that your husband is a Christian, but put some thought into what other spiritual and character qualities are important.

When you are finished, pray about your list. Ask God to bring His choice for your husband into your life at the right time. Commit to wait until God brings him to you instead of getting into relationships with guys who aren't God's best for your life. Be sure to tell God that you will submit to His plan for your life whether it does or does not include a husband. Tell Him you realize no one but Christ can truly satisfy your need for love. We'll provide more for you on that topic tomorrow.

QUALITIES I MOST DESIRE IN A HUSBAND

Career man
- Sincere and delicate
- Pretty eyes :)
- Omniscient
- Manage his finance good / Good management in finan
- Family person
- European — Have the most powerful passport
- Taller than me
- Wealthy
- Kind-hearted
- Supportive
- Know how to dress
- [Gojo Satoru]
- Strong / Physique
- Persistent

Tough will / Fighter
Funny
Gentle
babygirl - 13h side
organized
Thoughtful
Caring
artistic
play guitar
Man Gestures
Small detail
Patient
Dog any animal love
[except!!! bugs]

68

I Need a Boyfriend

 READ

Read Lie #10, "I need a boyfriend," in *LYWB* (pages 91–96).

 REALIZE

Since this lie can be rooted in several lines of deception, today's Realize section is a little different. We'll be driving you into the Word to search for Truth on three important concepts:

1. Letting Christ satisfy

2. Understanding God's purpose for marriage

3. Waiting for God's timing

LETTING CHRIST SATISFY

What do the following verses tell us about our ability to find satisfaction anywhere but in Christ? Jot down your thoughts on each verse:

✦ Psalm 37:4 _Delight yourself in the Lord, and he will give you the desires of your heart. → Build faith in him, the Lord, then your desires shall be granted._

✦ Psalm 103:1-5 _Praise the Lord, and forget not all his benefits. → Praise and grateful be_

✦ Psalm 146 _Praise the Lord_

✦ John 4:13-14 _Jesus answered, 'Everyone who drinks this water will be thirsty again, but whoever drinks the water I give him will never thirst._

Those verses tell us that we have needs that Christ alone is able to satisfy. What are those needs?

Lon Meditate

UNDERSTANDING GOD'S PURPOSE FOR MARRIAGE

Look up Ephesians 5:25–33. What do these verses tell us about God's purpose for marriage?

Respect for each other

God created marriage, in part, to be a picture of Christ's love for the church. Amazing, isn't it? Your future marriage, if that is what God has planned for you, has the potential to be a portrait of the greatest relationship that exists. It's that holy!

WAITING FOR GOD'S TIMING

Look up Song of Solomon 2:7. What does this verse tell us about God's timing for our dating relationships?

I charge you, by the roses, and by the hinds of the field, that ye stir not up, nor awake my love, till he pleases

We are told to not "awaken love" until it is time—not to fuel romantic or sexual desires until those can be legitimately fulfilled in the context of marriage.

1. Combining your notes on all three of these important areas, why do you think that the lie "I need a boyfriend" could be dangerous?

[lies young women believe]

💬 **2. In *LYWB* we wrote about a young woman who did something drastic to break the boy-crazy phase of her life.** She decided to spend a year focusing on God rather than guys. Each weekend, she spent one evening with God instead of on dates. In just two months, she was not as consumed with guys. How would your life be different if you took similar steps?

Be more confident, Faith ↑ and love myself more <3

R RESPOND

1. Psalm 146:3 reminds us not to put our hope in princes. Have you been disappointed before when you have looked to a "Prince Charming" to satisfy the deepest longings of your heart? Write about that experience here.

Absolutely.
Me being delusional ☺

💬 **2. Are there any specific boundaries that you think it would be wise to establish in your dating life as a result of this study?** What are they?

No clinginess (lesser the better)
Everyone needs their own privacy
Either Partners   social life

PRAY ABOUT IT

Jesus, thank You for the gift of marriage. Help me wait for Your timing for this type of relationship. Help me find satisfaction in You instead of in dating relationships. Specifically, show me how I can glorify You in this season of my life, and help me look to You to meet my need for . . .

happiness,
family

It's Not Really Sex

 READ

Read Lie #11, "It's not really sex" in *LYWB* (pages 96–100).

 REALIZE

1. When it comes to sex, you may wonder, "How far is too far?" God sets a solid, easy-to-understand standard for purity for us in Ephesians 5:3 (NIV). Look it up and read it. Then, fill in the blank.

God requires that you and I have not even a ___*hint*___ of sexual impurity in our lives.

The real question isn't "How far is too far?" but rather, "How can I avoid even a hint of sexual impurity?"

2. There are many ways to hint at sexual sin. You have complicated relationship status', entertainment choices, and the constant influence of the Internet to navigate. Write three specific examples of "hinting" at sexual sin that you see around you.

1. ... b4 marriage
2. abortion
3.

3. Read Matthew 5:28. In this verse, Jesus points out that it is not just our actions that make us impure. What are some common influences that might lead to an impure thought life?

Whosoever looked on a woman to lust after her had committed adultery with her already in his heart

→ Lustful thoughts, unhealthy thinking about s* Hubits, seeing ppl doing things then they mimic
Peers   ll Ppl we hang out who we're with

R RESPOND *think, had to consider the consequences*

1. What standard of purity would you like your future husband to have? Consider your level of comfort when thinking about him flirting, lusting, or engaging in sexual activity with other girls. Write your thoughts below.

Good bye ye
So long → *Happy being single* ☺

If you are uncomfortable imagining your future husband "hinting" at sexual contact with girls through the activities you listed above, don't you think these are activities you should avoid as well? ✓

2. What are the rewards of refusing to engage in any sexual activity outside of marriage?

P PRAY ABOUT IT

Jesus, I want to follow Your standard for purity. I want to save every part of my heart and body for my husband. I realize that sometimes I "hint" at sexual sin when I . . .

see / hanging out w/ the people around me. However, I will not let that comes into my head. I do not have that kind of "desire" / "hint" @ sexual sin but I hope others would realee that and they all can be saved from bad things. Amen.

[lies young women believe]

I Can't Handle the Loneliness of Staying Pure

R READ

Read Lie #12, "I can't handle the loneliness of staying pure," in *LYWB* (pages 100–103).

R REALIZE

💬 **1. In *LYWB*, Dannah shared her story of falling into sexual sin as a teenager.** After the sin, she experienced extreme loneliness. Have you ever witnessed that kind of loneliness in someone's life after they gave in to sexual sin? Without using names, describe what you observed.

💬 **2. In what ways might someone face loneliness while standing for purity and waiting for God's best?**

----

3. Loneliness is a painful and powerful emotion. Let's examine the guidance Scripture offers for dealing with this particular feeling. Fill in the blanks for the following verses.

❧ *"I will _____ _____ _____ nor _____ you."* (HEBREWS 13:5)

❧ *"And behold, ____ _____ _____ _____ _____,*
     to the _____ of the _____." (MATTHEW 28:20)

❧ *"Cast all your _____ on _____ because _____ _____*
         for _____." (1 PETER 5:7 NIV)

What specific promises do these verses offer to help us handle loneliness?

----

4. What advice would you have given to the girl we quoted in *LYWB* who said she wonders if she is going to wait because she feels so alone?

_____

_____

R RESPOND

1. Circle any items on this list that create pressure for you to give in to sexual behavior. Next to each one explain what causes that pressure.

- Boyfriend _____
- Friends _____
- Netflix _____
- Music _____
- School _____
- Social Media _____
- Other _____

2. What specific boundaries can you place in your life to limit the influence of these sources?

_____

_____

_____

3. Who do you have in your life who is encouraging you to pursue purity?

_____

If you can't think of anyone who's helping you, it's time to change that! Find someone older and wiser to encourage you in the quest to remain pure. Ask them to be your accountability partner specifically in the area of sexual purity.

ⓟ PRAY ABOUT IT

Jesus, thank You for Your promise that You will never leave me. Help me remember that the loneliness I feel now is worth the reward of remaining pure until marriage. Help me turn to You when I am tempted to . . .

ⒶⒸⓉ ACT Make a prayer box for your husband. Write out your prayers to God about your future marriage and mate. Tell God your desires. Pray for God's blessing on your future husband's life. Pray that he will be growing and maturing spiritually in preparation for your marriage. Ask God to keep him pure until your wedding day. Place those written prayers in a special place to one day share with your future husband.

When you're tempted to settle for anything less than God's best in this area of your life, take your prayers out and read them. You'll be encouraged to stay the course. On your wedding day, you will be astounded by the ways that God has faithfully answered your prayers. **You might even consider giving your prayer box to your husband as a testimony of God's faithfulness in this area of your life.**

Lies About Relationships

This week, you'll read chapter 8: Lies About Relationships in _LYWB_.

Catching a Glimpse

{ "We found that many professing _Christian_ girls we talked to were likely to gossip, use mild to wild profanity, talk casually about things like sex or menstruation with guys, be mean to teens outside of their peer group, and post or look at mild sexual photos _when they were online_. (Though you'd never dream of doing that at home or at church!) The Internet offers you a place to be someone you are not in person." }

(_Lies Young Women Believe_, page 110)

KNOW the TRUTH

Here's some powerful Truth for you to memorize this week:

"Greater love has no one than this, that someone lay down his life for his friends. You are my friends if you do what I command you. No longer do I call you servants, for the servant does not know what his master is doing; but I have called you friends, for all that I have heard from my Father I have made known to you."

(JOHN 15:13–15)

DAY ONE:
Finding Balance

READ

To lay the foundation for this week's study, we're going to head back to chapter 1. Reread Lie #1, "God is not enough" in *LYWB* (pages 42–44).

REALIZE

1. A whopping 88 percent of the girls who participated in our focus groups admitted that they believed the lie that God is not enough. Look back over their direct quotes. Where were they most prone to seek satisfaction outside of a relationship with God?

peers , friends @ school or any place

The girls we interviewed said that they couldn't live without their *friends*. While many types of relationships aren't inherently bad, we get in trouble when we begin to lean on them too much.

2. It is possible for our relationships to become idols when our devotion gets off balance. Let's take a look at what Scripture says about idols. Look up the following verses and write them in your own words below.

❖ 1 Samuel 12:21 *Don't turn away after useless idols*

❖ Psalm 135:15–18 *Choose wisely to follow*

❖ Psalm 106:36 *They served their idols, which became a snare to them*

✦ 1 John 5:21 _keep little children away from idols_

3. Many of the verses in the Bible that warn against idol worship are referring to the practice of worshiping an *object* believed to have supernatural powers. (Remember the golden calf the Israelites worshiped in Exodus 32?) That's not exactly what we're talking about here, but it is possible to misdirect our worship and affection toward a person or relationship. List three signs that we are leaning too heavily on our human relationships.

✦ **1.** _Job / Occupation prospectives_
✦ **2.**
✦ **3.**

R RESPOND

1. What relationships are the most important to you? List five.

✦ **1.** _Family_
✦ **2.** _Health_
✦ **3.** _Friends_ — _(can interchange ☺)_
✦ **4.** _Work_
✦ **5.** _Travel ☺_

2. Look back over the list you just made. Circle any relationships that you look to for satisfaction, security, or purpose more than you look to Christ.

💬 **3. Many of the girls in our focus groups told us that they need their friends more than God.** This is evidence of the widespread belief that God is not enough and that we can be satisfied by friends. Based on what you've observed in your own life and the lives of others, how do you think that believing this lie can cause harm?

 **PRAY ABOUT IT**

Jesus, I know that You are able to satisfy my needs. I realize that I rely too heavily on my relationship with . . .

friends I met and family I love. I know it's good to have them around me but I always feel anxious when I'm on my own. However, I have changed. With You, dear Father, I know I can be tough and strong on my own. I am grateful for You. Amen

DAY TWO:

It's OK to Be One Person at Home and a Different Person with Others ... Especially Online

READ

Read the introduction to chapter 8 and Lie #13, "It's OK to be one person at home and a different person with others ... especially online," in *LYWB* (pages 109–13).

REALIZE

1. The girls in our focus groups told us they hate hypocrisy. This came up a lot in our discussions about faith and church. After reading this chapter, how would you define the term *hypocrite*?

liars, deceived, fake

A hypocrite is someone whose actions are different from his or her stated beliefs.

2. Let's look at how Jesus responded to hypocrites. Write down how each of the following verses describes His response.

Matthew 23:25–26 what's inside is important then the outside

Mark 12:13–15 Pay no attention to who they are but you teach the way of God in accordance w/ the truth

Luke 12:1 Be on your guard against the yeast of the Pharisees, which is hypocrisy

3. Based on what you just read, how do you think Jesus would respond to your social media profiles and posts?

Calm ☺ I don't post much

R RESPOND

1. Have you ever helped your mom with spring cleaning? If so, then you know to look in closets, drawers, corners, and under the refrigerator for trash, dust bunnies, or items that are out of place. Today it's time for you to do a different kind of housecleaning project. We're going to search online (assuming it's OK with your parents!). Specifically, you're going to dig through *your* social-media profiles, text-message history, and email inbox. Circle any of the following items you find *on your personal profiles and history* (do *not* go looking anywhere else!).

- a profile picture that is mildly sexual
- a photo of you kissing a guy
- profanity
- drug paraphernalia or references
- negative comments about other people
- dialogue that is sexual in nature
- negative comments about an authority

- use of God's name in vain
- photos obviously taken at parties (specifically those involving alcohol)
- links to YouTube videos with questionable content
- mean-girl comments

2. Is the image you project online different than the image you project at home or at church? Is your profile consistent with what you say you believe about God? What specific changes do you need to make to avoid being hypocritical?

No

IdK

_____ Bad things ☹ Oh, be more careful _____

_____

3. Find someone to hold you accountable. Ask an older, wiser woman to take a look at your social-media profile and messaging history. If you are already cringing at the thought, this exercise is likely a good tool for exposing areas of hypocrisy in your life. This could be your youth pastor's wife, an older sibling, or your mom. Ask them to help you see areas where you are not guarding your heart or your words and end up acting differently in different settings. Give them access to your online communication so they can warn you when you seem to be slipping and permission to lovingly correct you when you've allowed yourself to return to old habits.

[lies young women believe]

P PRAY ABOUT IT

Jesus, help me honor You with every area of my life. Give me wisdom to recognize when the things I say or do contradict the person You are calling me to be. I know that I need to get rid of hypocrisy in the area of . . .

life :)

If I Just Had Friends, I Wouldn't Be So Lonely

 ## READ

Read Lie #14, "If I just had friends, I wouldn't be so lonely," in *LYWB* (pages 113–16).

 ## REALIZE

1. In *LYWB* we reminded you of two vital Truths that can help you overcome this lie about friendship:

    1. Each of us is created with a God-shaped hole within us.

    2. We were created to know God and to be His friend.

How do these two statements help explain our craving for friendship?

To be intergrated! We have God, his spirit live in us. We are His friend but only in spiritually → We need friendship!

We were created for intimacy with God; but instead of pursuing friendship with Him, we often try to fill that "God-shaped hole" with human friendships. It never works, at least not for long.

When we seek God first, we are able to have our deepest needs met, giving us freedom to enjoy friendship without idolizing our friends.

We've already looked at the importance of spending time with God. Now let's focus on learning to treat our friends like God treats us.

2. Read John 15:12–17. Verse 16 reminds us who took the initiative in this friendship. Fill in the blanks.

    ✤ *"You did not _____ me, but I _____ you."*

When we were not pursuing Him—in fact, when we were His enemies—He sought us out, extended His love to us, and drew us into a relationship with Him. Now He calls us His friends and wants to enjoy close friendship with us!

Do you tend to initiate connection with new friends or do you wait for others to reach out to you?

3. Jesus chose us. (Not the other way around.) That's something we often don't model well in our earthly relationships. We get consumed with who likes us and who might pick us as a friend, rather than looking for who needs a friend! Look up the following verses and jot down some insights into being a good friend.

Proverbs 18:24 _____

_____

Proverbs 17:17 _____

_____

Proverbs 27:6 _____

_____

R RESPOND

1. If you shifted your focus away from having more friends and toward *being* a friend to others who need you, how would it specifically change your life? How it would impact your time, your emotions, and your actions?

_____

_____

_____

_____

_____

_____

_____

_____

2. What are three practical ways you can be a better friend?

_____

_____

_____

P PRAY ABOUT IT

Dear God, it is amazing to consider that You—the God of the universe—created me to be Your friend. When I think about this I feel . . .

I'm My Own Authority

READ

Read Lie #15, "I'm my own authority," in *LYWB* (pages 116–21).

REALIZE

1. There are a lot of lies tucked under the lie "I'm my own authority." We listed three in this chapter. Do you identify with any of these lies? Write your honest feelings about each of them below.

1. "I only need to submit if I agree with my authorities."

_____

_____

_____

_____

_____

2. "I can't express my thoughts or my opinions to my authorities."

_____

_____

_____

_____

_____

3. "My authorities are always right."

_____

_____

_____

_____

_____

2. Read the following verses and summarize what they reveal about God's perspective on authority.

✤ Ephesians 5:21 _____

_____

✤ Colossians 3:18–24 _____

_____

✤ Hebrews 13:17 _____

_____

✤ Romans 13:1–7 _____

_____

✤ 1 Peter 2:13–17 _____

3. The Bible contains many stories of individuals who resisted submitting to authority. Let's look at one example. Check out Jonah's rebellion in Jonah 1–2. What were the consequences of Jonah's failure to submit to God's authority?

_____

_____

_____

Failing to submit to God always ends in disaster. Maybe not right away. (Perhaps it was a sunny day at sea the first day Jonah set out on his cruise away from God's plan.) But eventually. (Three days inside that big fish was no party!)

4. Who appoints all human authority according to Romans 13:1?

_____

Based on your answer, whose authority are we ultimately disobeying when we disobey earthly authorities?

We are ultimately disobeying _____.

 **RESPOND**

1. Who are your human authorities? Write five of them below.

1. _____

2. _____

3. _____

4. _____

5. _____

2. Circle the names above that you sometimes struggle to submit to. Then, get specific and write what disrespectful things you do. This may be painful, but it is a good exercise!

_____

_____

_____

_____

_____

_____

What specific changes does God want you to make to be obedient to the authorities He has placed in your life?

_____

_____

_____

3. We don't want to discount the fact that sometimes our authorities are wrong. And sometimes those authorities who are wrong are our parents. Look at page 119 in *LYWB* if you have an area where you find it difficult to submit to your parents because you believe they are wrong. Read the sidebar about "How to Respond to Parents When You Don't Agree with Their Decisions." Select one of the six ideas to put into practice today. Write about it below.

_____

_____

_____

_____

📍 PRAY ABOUT IT

Father, I am thankful that I can trust Your authority. Help me surrender my life and will to You, especially in the area of . . .

A ACT Grab a friend and write letters to your parents. We know that talking honestly with your parents can be a challenge. To help open lines of communication, write a letter to your parents, thanking them for all they do for you. Don't go at it alone. Enlist a Christian friend to help. Give each other ideas of what to say and how to say it. You might think about including a list of all the ways your parents provide for you, things you appreciate about each parent, or insight into the ways your parents help you spiritually. Read each other's letters before giving them to your parents. Be open to suggestions. **This will be a great way to create some accountability in this area, and we're almost sure your parents will be blown away! They'll feel honored, and God will be pleased.**

Lies About My Faith

This week, you'll read chapter 9: Lies about My Faith in *LYWB*.

Catching a Glimpse

{

"The church is God's plan; Jesus loves it and gave
His life for it. It may be tempting to cut yourself off when the
going gets rough, but as a part of God's spiritual family,
He hasn't given us the option of 'dropping out.'"

}

(*Lies Young Women Believe*, page 130)

KNOW the TRUTH

Here's a verse that will help you to process an essential doctrine of the Christian faith. Hide it in your heart this week:

"If you confess with your mouth that
Jesus is Lord and believe in your heart that
God raised him from the dead, you will
be saved. For with the heart one believes
and is justified, and with the mouth one
confesses and is saved."

(ROMANS 10:9–10)

A Look at the Church

 READ

Read the introduction for chapter 9 in *LYWB* (pages 127–28).

✺ REALIZE

1. Luke writes about the early church in the book of Acts. Write out Acts 2:42–47 below.

---

2. Look over that passage again and circle the purposes of the church that are mentioned.
(Example: fellowship)

3. Look up Hebrews 10:24–25. Fill in the blanks below.

>> *"And let us consider how to _____ ____ _____ _____*

to _____ and _____ _____,

not _____ to _____ _____,

as is the habit of some, but _____ _____ _____,

and all the more as you see the Day drawing near."

We need regular fellowship with other believers. The local church is designed by God to meet this need.

4. During our focus groups, we noticed that many young women responded to lies about faith by attending church less frequently or abandoning church entirely. What advice would you give to these girls to convince them not to abandon a connection to a local church? Use at least one Scripture to back up your thoughts.

R RESPOND

1. Do you have a testimony about a time when your church family cared for your needs or the needs of your family? Write about one experience below.

---

2. What role has your church played in the development of your faith?

----

3. What could be some of the negative effects on your spiritual life when you attend church less often or not at all?

ⓟ PRAY ABOUT IT

Jesus, thank You for the church. I realize that I need other believers to help me to . . .

[lies young women believe]

DAY TWO:
My Youth Pastor Is My Connection to God

R READ

Read Lie #16, "My youth pastor is my connection to God," in *LYWB* (pages 128–30).

R REALIZE

1. Look up Hebrews 9:1–7. This chapter is explaining the practices of God's people before the crucifixion of Christ. According to verse 7, what was required for God's people to receive forgiveness for their sins before the new covenant?

_____

_____

The high priest offered sacrifices on behalf of the people. He was the only one who could enter directly into God's presence. He did this on behalf of all the people. He was their "mediator"— the one assigned to go between God and the people.

2. Now look up Hebrews 9:15 and 1 Timothy 2:5–6 to see how the high priest's role changed after Christ's death. According to these verses, who is the only mediator between God and us?

_____

3. Think back to Dannah's conversation with Courtney in the introduction of this chapter. Why do you think Courtney and many of the other girls we've talked to reacted so strongly when they were wounded by the decisions of their youth pastor?

_____

_____

Many of the girls we interviewed seemed to be looking to their youth pastors or leaders as "mediators" rather than advisors, teachers, and mentors. Some of you have witnessed some pretty bad youth pastor exits. That hurts, but we were really shocked at the depth of the hurt. Something is off base. Perhaps it's simply recognizing the true role of a youth pastor. He's not your mediator.

[lies about my faith]   99

⟦R⟧ RESPOND

1. What role does your youth pastor play in the development of your faith? Select one below that best reflects your answer:

A. He's my connection to God! (I don't do a lot of personal Bible study. I get most of my spiritual food from him!)

B. He's been the reason I'm disconnected from God!
(I was really hurt when he _____.)

C. He's one of many spiritual mentors in my life, but Jesus is my connection to God.

💬 **2. Based on your answer above and the information you've read in this chapter, do you feel like your relationship with your youth pastor is healthy and balanced?** Write about your reasoning below.

_____

_____

_____

_____

_____

_____

💬 **3. What consequences have you seen in your own life or the lives of your friends when relationships with spiritual mentors are unbalanced?**

_____

_____

_____

_____

_____

4. Those in church authority have a tough job! And while they aren't meant to be our connection to God, they can play an important role in the development of our faith and Christian walk. Do something encouraging for the leadership at your church. Here are a few ideas to get you started:

- Write a thank-you note.

- Stop by the church office with a milkshake or cup of coffee.

- Make a video about some of the ways your pastor or youth pastor have positively impacted your life.

PRAY ABOUT IT

Jesus, thank You for dying for me. Thank You for paying the price for my sin so that I no longer need a priest to mediate on my behalf. I realize that sometimes I elevate my spiritual leaders to a position reserved for You. This is especially true when . . .

DAY THREE:
Everyone at Church is Judging Me

R READ

Read Lie #17, "Everyone at church is judging me," from *LYWB* (pages 130–33).

R REALIZE

1. Look up the following verses and summarize them in your own words. Pay close attention to what each verse tells us about the church.

✦ Ephesians 1:22–23 _____

_____

_____

✦ Ephesians 5:25–27 _____

_____

_____

2. Let's take a closer look at one of the quotes highlighted in this chapter.

"A support group for alcoholics meets at our church on Sundays right before we come back for evening activities. You should have heard the uproar when that decision was made. They're not the cleanest bunch. They smoke in the parking lot, and that really ruffled some feathers. Here's a group of people being real about their need, and the one place that's supposed to welcome them—the place that has the Answer—is too busy fighting over whether they should meet here or not. Do you think I'd ever talk about my sin? No way!" (*Lies Young Women Believe,* page 131).

Imagine that this was a friend of yours who was talking about her frustration with her own church. Write out the advice you would offer her based on what you've read in this chapter.

_____

_____

_____

_____

3. Now look for a specific Scripture that would enrich your counsel to your friend. Write it below.

⟦R⟧ RESPOND

1. Have you ever felt judged by the people at your church? Write about one specific experience.

----

2. As you look back at that experience, what were the underlying emotions you felt at the time?
(For example: hurt or embarrassed)

----

3. Based on the advice you offered your imaginary friend in the Realize section above, what is the best way to respond when you are feeling judged?

 **PRAY ABOUT IT**

Jesus, thank You for the church. Help me develop a love for the church and for Your
people. I now realize that at times I have been judgmental toward others, especially . . .

[lies young women believe]

DAY FOUR:
Of Course I'm a Christian, I . . .

 READ

Read Lie #18, "Of course I'm a Christian, I . . ." in *LYWB* (pages 134–37).

 REALIZE

1. Look over the list of "of course" statements we presented in *LYWB*. Circle any that you believed at one time or may still believe today.

Of course I'm a Christian . . .

- I go to church all the time.
- my parents are Christians.
- I grew up in church.
- I went forward during a service.
- my mom told me that I prayed to receive Christ when I was three!

Would it surprise you to know that any or all of the above could be true, and you could still not be a true Christian? So how can you know for sure? God's Word shows us how.

2. Look at the summary of the verses from 1 John on page 135 in *LYWB*. In the left column below, write the characteristics of a genuine Christian that you consistently live out. Write the ones you struggle with in the right column.

YES, I AM . . .

_____

_____

_____

_____

NO, I'M NOT . . .

_____

_____

_____

_____

3. If you are a Christian, the Bible says that the Holy Spirit will confirm it for you (Romans 8:16). Pray and ask God to show you that you are His!

4. What do the following verses tell us about what's necessary to become a follower of Christ? Write your answer next to each verse.

Ephesians 2:8–9 _____

_____

Romans 10:9–10 _____

_____

Acts 3:19 _____

_____

2 Corinthians 5:17 _____

5. Think back to Tish's story from this chapter. What took place during her conversation with Dannah in the diner that resulted in a radical change in her behavior?

_____

6. Some people think that being a Christian means following a bunch of rules and doing the right things. Read Matthew 7:21–23. In verse 22, Jesus talks about people who think they will get into heaven because they have done all sorts of religious works. What does He say about His relationship with those people in verse 23?

_____

_____

7. Read Romans 3:21–28. What are the key words or concepts in this passage that describe what it means to be a Christian?

_____

_____

R RESPOND

1. Have you had an encounter with Jesus Christ that forever changed you?
Write your testimony below.

If you have never had a life-changing encounter with Christ, why not do so right now! Use the prayer on page 136 of *LYWB*, or page 61 of this book as your guide. Then tell someone! Ask your pastor, youth pastor, parent, or mentor to pray with you and walk you through your next steps as a new believer.

2. What advice would you offer a friend who was struggling to know whether she was really a Christian? Write your thoughts below. Be sure to use Scripture along with your own thoughts.

----

3. Being a follower of Jesus isn't about making checklists of things to do or not do. It's not about being perfect either. True faith is about loving Him, worshiping Him, trusting in Him, and living your life for Him.

Ask the Lord to give you a love for Jesus that surpasses your love for anything or anyone else. Then take a few minutes to write out some of the things you love about the Lord.

PRAY ABOUT IT

Dear God, thank You for making a way for me to be forgiven of my sins and to be in fellowship with You. I know that I am saved because . . .

ACT Interview your pastor. Your pastor is probably an expert when it comes to the consequences of believing lies about faith. He has likely counseled many people who are struggling through these or similar issues. Ask if he and his wife could set aside some time to talk with you about what they have experienced. We've given you some ideas for possible questions and left room for you to write their responses:

What lies about Christianity do you see people believing?

_____

_____

_____

What advice do you give individuals who are in bondage because of those lies?

_____

_____

_____

What impact do these lies have on the church body?

_____

_____

_____

What Scriptures do you use to combat these lies?

_____

_____

_____

Lies About Sin

This week, you'll read chapter 10: Lies about Sin in *LYWB* (pages 143–53).

Catching a Glimpse

{
"The initial point of salvation, which the Bible calls our *justification*, is followed by a lifelong process that the Bible calls *sanctification*. That's an important theological word that has to do with becoming more and more like Jesus in every area of your life."

(*Lies Young Women Believe*, page 143).
}

KNOW the TRUTH

Do you have any verses about sin in your tool box of Truth? Here's one to store up!

"We know that our old self was crucified with him in order that the body of sin might be brought to nothing, so that we would no longer be enslaved to sin. For one who has died has been set free from sin."

(ROMANS 6:6–7)

Understanding Sin

 ## READ

You don't have to read anything new in *LYWB* today. We're going to lay a foundation for the next lie, which we'll look at on Day Two.

 ## REALIZE

1. How would you define sin? Write your answer below.

----

2. As we prepare to tackle specific lies about sin, we need to make sure that you know what sin is. Does that sound too elementary? It probably won't if we go back to the Hebrew language!

Chatá is one of the Hebrew words for sin in the Old Testament. It originally meant to miss the mark. Think of it like a marksman would. With a bow and arrow in hand he releases an arrow toward the target and then. . . *chatá*! He misses the bull's-eye.

Let's apply this to our definition of sin. When we sin, what mark do we miss? What is our bull's eye?

3. Often the result of our sin is a lot of hard work! This is easy to see in Adam's and Eve's lives. Can you think of another example from Scripture where sin made things more difficult for the offender(s)? Write about it below.

One of the clearest examples of this principle is the wandering of the Israelites found in Numbers and Deuteronomy. God provided all that the Israelites needed to enter the Promised Land but they missed the mark. As a result they toiled for forty years in the desert.

4. Let's combine these two definitions to create a definition of sin we can easily apply to our own lives. Fill in the blanks below.

>>
    ✤ Sin is _____

    ✤ The result in my life is _____

R RESPOND

1. Think back to a recent time when you made a sinful choice. Relate that choice to the concepts of sin above:

✤ I recently made the sinful choice to _____.

✤ As a result I missed the mark of God's design for my life. God's best for me in this situation was _____. Instead, I received _____. As a result my life was made more difficult in this way: _____.

2. What are some consequences that we always face when we sin, whether we realize it or not? Write two or three. (Isaiah 59:2 will get you started.)

_____

_____

_____

P PRAY ABOUT IT

Father, I know that when I sin I miss the mark of Your design for my life. As a result I miss out on Your best for me. I realize that I am missing the mark in the area of . . .

_____

_____

_____

_____

_____

DAY TWO:
I Can't Overcome My Sin

R READ

Read the introduction to chapter 10 and Lie #19, "I can't overcome my sin," in *LYWB* (pages 143–46).

R REALIZE

1. The Bible talks about being "slaves to sin" (see John 8:34; Romans 6:16–17). What does it mean to be "enslaved"? What does it mean to be enslaved to sin?

_____

_____

It's true that we cannot break free from our sin on our own. But the devil wants us to believe that means we can never be set free from certain sins that have enslaved us. God's Word offers liberating Truth to counteract this lie. Let's take a look.

2. Fill in the blanks for the following passages

✤ "For the _____ of _____ has appeared, bringing _____ for

_____ _____, _____ _____ to _____ _____

and _____ _____, and to live _____,

_____, and _____ lives in the present age." (TITUS 2:11–12)

According to these verses what does the grace of God train us to do?

✤ "So you also must consider yourselves _____ to _____ and _____

to _____ in Christ Jesus. Let not _____ therefore _____ in your _____ _____,

to make you _____ its _____. _____ _____ _____ your

_____ to _____ as _____ for _____,

but _____ _____ to _____ as those who have been brought

from _____ to _____, and your members to God as _____ for _____.

For _____ will have ____ _____ over you, since you are not under

_____ but under _____." (ROMANS 6:11–14)

What do you think this phrase means: "sin will have no dominion over you"?

_____

3. According to this passage, what has made it possible for us to be free from sin?

_____

_____

4. Think back to Tish's story. She was trapped in a pattern of sexual sin even though she desperately *wanted* to change. What was it about her conversation with Dannah in the diner that led to her receiving true freedom in this area?

_____

_____

R RESPOND

💬 **1. What sinful attitudes or behaviors have you found difficult to overcome?**

_____

_____

2. Think about your response to the question above. Do you truly agree with God that the things you mentioned are sins, or do you secretly think there's really nothing wrong with what you're doing?

_____

_____

3. Romans 6:13 tells us not to offer the parts of our bodies to sin. For example, we offer our tongue to sin when we use it for lying or gossip. We offer our mind to sin when we use it for lustful fantasies. Instead, we are to offer ourselves to God. How can you use these and other parts of your body to glorify God instead of sinning?

_____

_____

4. What are some practical ways you can remind yourself to rely on the grace of God and the power of the Holy Spirit to resist temptation?

P PRAY ABOUT IT

Father, thank You for forgiving me and setting me free from sin. I need Your grace to say no to certain sins that I am tempted to give in to. I especially desire to overcome my sin in the area of . . .

[lies young women believe]

In Certain Situations It's Okay to Break the Law or Rules if I'm Not Hurting Myself or Others

READ

Read Lie #20, "In certain situations it's okay to break the law or rules if I'm not hurting myself or others," in *LYWB* (pages 147–49).

REALIZE

1. Look up the following passages. What does each one tell us about the consequences of sin?

❖ Psalm 51:3 _____

_____

❖ Psalm 51:12 _____

_____

❖ Proverbs 28:1 _____

_____

❖ Isaiah 59:1–2 _____

_____

❖ Ephesians 4:30 _____

_____

❖ 1 Thessalonians 5:19 _____

_____

2. What consequences did Eve face as a result of her sin?

_____

3. Consider the story of the young college student who was ultimately sentenced to prison as a result of his sin. In addition to a prison sentence, what consequences did he likely face? Refer back to the list of consequences you outlined above to get you started.

_____

_____

_____

_____

_____

 # RESPOND

1. Quiz time! Circle your answer to the following questions.

1. WHEN IS IT OKAY TO BREAK THE LAW?

> When no one gets hurt

> When the law is out of date or irrational

> When no one finds out

> Only when the law opposes God's law

2. RULES ARE . . .

> meant to be broken.

> just suggestions; you can follow them if you want to.

> supposed to be followed no matter what.

> it depends on the rule.

3. YOU'RE DRIVING HOME ON FRIDAY AND YOU ARE LATE FOR CURFEW. WHAT DO YOU DO?

> Speed! You'd rather risk the ticket than take a chance of getting grounded (again!).

> Stop and get ice cream. You're already late, why rush?

> Call your mom and apologize, then follow the speed limit all the way home.

> What's the big deal? You're always late for curfew.

In our discussion groups, more than 70 percent of the girls we interviewed said that in certain situations, it's OK to break the rules or the law. They said this was especially true when breaking the rules did not cause any harm to themselves or others. Do the answers you gave on the quiz above indicate that you think it's OK to break the rules in some situations?

[lies young women believe]

2. What are some rules you find difficult to obey? List three.

_____

_____

_____

3. What are some of the consequences of breaking the rules in your life? For example, maybe it strains your relationship with your parents or makes it difficult for your teachers to trust you.

_____

_____

_____

4. Read John 14:15, 23. What is the heart motivation for our obedience?

_____

PRAY ABOUT IT

God, I am thankful that You have established rules for my protection. Remind me of this truth when I am tempted to rebel in the area of . . .

_____

_____

_____

_____

_____

_____

_____

_____

_____

I Can't Control Myself When I'm Stressed or PMS-ing

READ

Read Lie #21, "I can't control myself when I'm stressed or PMS-ing,"
in *LYWB* (pages 149–51).

REALIZE

💬 **1. What do the following verses tell us about self-control?**

✤ Proverbs 16:32 _____

_____

✤ Proverbs 25:28 _____

_____

✤ Proverbs 29:11 _____

_____

✤ Galatians 5:22–23 _____

_____

✤ 2 Peter 1:5–8 _____

_____

2. Look up 2 Corinthians 10:5. Paraphrase it in your own words below.

_____

_____

_____

_____

3. What does it mean to "take every thought captive"?

_____

_____

4. Think back to the story of the girl whose PMS was so severe that she had to drop out of school for a season. She admitted that she was nasty to her friends and family when her hormones were raging. List two or three other ways we tend to act out when we are feeling out of control.

_____

_____

_____

5. Read 2 Timothy 1:7, 13–14. According to these verses, what (or who) can help us exercise self-control in our attitudes and behavior, even when our emotions feel out of control?

_____

R RESPOND

1. What causes you the most stress?

2. How do you typically respond to stress? Are these healthy or unhealthy responses?

3. How do you feel when you have PMS? List your physical and emotional symptoms below.

When I have PMS, _physically_ I feel _____

_____

_____

When I have PMS, _emotionally_ I feel _____

_____

_____

4. Can you think of a time when your PMS resulted in out of control behavior (such as the time Dannah threw her lunch at a teacher)? Write about your experience.

_____

_____

_____

_____

_____

_____

_____

_____

_____

_____

_____

_____

_____

CHART YOUR
PMS!

Chart your physical and emotional PMS symptoms for a few months. Use an app to make the process super easy! Pay close attention to symptoms that make you feel out of control such as irritability, weepiness, or over-the-top appetites for certain foods. Use this chart to help you see which areas you need to pray about and where you should seek guidance from Scripture.

5. What practical strategies can you put in place to help you gain control in the future? Especially focus on how you can depend on the Holy Spirit to give you self-control. List three.

_____

_____

_____

_____

P PRAY ABOUT IT

Lord, when I feel out of control, help me run to Your Truth. I especially need help learning to control my feelings of . . .

_____

_____

_____

[lies young women believe]

_____

_____

_____

_____

_____

_____

_____

_____

_____

_____

_____

_____

◢ ACT **Make a survival kit.** This should include specific Scriptures that help you focus on making right choices during the times when your hormones are raging and your stress is off the charts. If you struggle with being irritable during this time, write out some verses on peace. If you tend to get depressed when your hormones flare up, write down some Scriptures on joy. When you are facing out of control emotions, pull out these Scriptures and post them where you can meditate on them.

Lies About Media and Lies About the Future

This week, you'll read chapter 11: Lies about Media (pages 157–65), and chapter 12: Lies about the Future in *LYWB* (pages 169–77).

Catching a Glimpse

"No other generation has had so much technology at their disposal, and you love it. You don't hang out at the soda parlor like your great-grandparents did. You hang out in cyberspace. We don't believe that technology—whether used for social networking or entertainment—is inherently 'bad'; it has its benefits. We do believe that using it mindlessly is a huge danger zone. We want to make sure that you're controlling it and it's not controlling you."

(*Lies Young Women Believe*, page 158).

KNOW
the
TRUTH

Here's a great verse to have in your heart as you think through your media choices and your future:

"Finally, brothers, whatever is true, whatever is honorable, whatever is just, whatever is pure, whatever is lovely, whatever is commendable, if there is any excellence, if there is anything worthy of praise, think about these things."

(PHILIPPIANS 4:8)

The Benefits of Constant Media Use Outweigh the Harm

R READ

Read the introduction to chapter 11 and Lie #22, "The benefits of constant media use outweigh the harm," in *LYWB* (pages 157–61).

R REALIZE

1. Look up the following verses and summarize them in your own words below.

✛ James 1:27 _____

_____

✛ James 4:4 _____

_____

✛ 1 John 2:15–17 _____

_____

✛ Romans 12:1–2 _____

_____

✛ Colossians 3:2 _____

_____

2. What common theme do you see in these verses?

_____

_____

Each of these verses urges us to avoid a love affair with the world. We'll explore what this looks like in the next section.

3. What do these verses tell us about the world's influence in our lives as Christians?

_ _

_ _

James 4:4 goes so far as to say that if we are a "friend of the world," that makes us "an enemy of God." That's a strong statement! Guarding our hearts against the mindset of the world is serious business. This can be especially true when we consider our media choices.

4. A whopping 98 percent of the girls we talked to admitted that their media choices negatively affected their relationship with God and others. What Scriptures would you cite to convince them that their media choices matter? Write two below.

_ _

_ _

R RESPOND

1. The media we expose ourselves to impacts our thoughts and feelings. Music is particularly powerful!

Write the name of a song beside each of the following emotions:

"_____" makes me happy.

"_____" makes me want to work out!

"_____" makes me sad.

"_____" makes me remember _____.

Looking at the list above, do you agree or disagree that you are affected by your media choices? Defend your position!

_ _

_ _

_ _

_ _

2. We need to learn to think about our media choices, rather than mindlessly taking in whatever is most popular. Make a list of your top three favorite choices in each of these categories:

❧ Television shows

1. _____

2. _____

3. _____

❧ Songs or musical artists

1. _____

2. _____

3. _____

❧ Movies

1. _____

2. _____

3. _____

❧ Pages I follow on social media

1. _____

2. _____

3. _____

>> **We invite you to follow us on social media:** @LiesYoungWomenBelieve on Instagram, @LYWBblog on Twitter. Sometimes it's good to have a little reminder in there about God's truth, and we'll be faithful to provide that to you!

3. Take a critical look at one of your faves listed above. Evaluate this specific choice using the guidelines on page 163 of *LYWB*.

_____

_____

Based on your list, is this media choice having a positive or negative effect on your spiritual life?

 **PRAY ABOUT IT**

Jesus, help me value my relationship with You above everything else, including my media. I realize that I need to be more mindful of my media habits, especially . . .

It's Not a Waste of Time... Even If It Is, It's OK

R READ

Read Lie #23, "It's not a waste of time . . . even if it is, it's OK," in *LYWB* (pages 161–63).

R REALIZE

1. Fill in the blanks for the following verse.

✤ *"Look _____ then how you _____, not as _____*

but as _____, making the _____ _____ of the _____, because the

_____ are _____. Therefore ____ _____ ___ _____,

but understand what the _____ of the _____ is." (Ephesians 5:15–17)

2. How can this passage be applied to the amount of time you spend plugged in to various media sources?

This passage encourages us to live wisely by making the best use of our time. This includes our media choices!

3. In this section, Nancy shared about her need to control her use of technology and social media. (It's not just young women who struggle with these issues!) Can you think of other examples of media-related activities that aren't always the best use of our time? Write two.

----

4. Think back to the story of Eve and the serpent in the garden. Her sinful choice was the result of listening to and dwelling on lies. How can our media choices be used to influence us to sin?

▣ RESPOND

1. Using the log below, fill in how much time you spend each day watching Netflix, talking on the phone, texting, and online. Also keep a record of how much time you spend in Bible reading and prayer. Keep track of your activities in each category for the next week.

	NETFLIX/TV	TALKING ON PHONE	TEXTING	ONLINE	BIBLE READING/PRAYER
Sunday					
Monday					
Tuesday					
Wednesday					
Thursday					
Friday					
Saturday					

About how many hours are you spending weekly using media?

2. How much time did you spend each day reading the Bible and praying? Compare the time you invest in media to the time you spend with God. Do these numbers seem balanced?

💬 **3. Many of the girls we interviewed recognize that there is imbalance in this area of their life, but weren't willing to do anything about it.** Why do you think this is the case?

4. Ask yourself the questions posed in the sidebar on page 163 of *LYWB*. Would you be embarrassed to watch it with Jesus? Does it create conflict between you and your parents? Is it something you have to hide? Does it cause you to isolate yourself from friends and family members? Does it cause you to neglect responsibilities? Are you addicted? Based on your answers, are there areas where you need to make adjustments in order to better align your life with biblical principles? What specific steps can you take to make these adjustments?

_____

_____

_____

_____

PRAY ABOUT IT

Lord Jesus, help me set limits in every area of my life, especially in the area of media. Help me use my time to glorify You. I realize that I need to change the amount of time I spend . . .

_____

_____

_____

_____

_____

_____

_____

_____

_____

_____

_____

[lies young women believe]

Having a Career Outside the Home Is More Valuable and Fulfilling Than Being "Just" a Wife and Mom

 READ

Read the introduction to chapter 12 and Lie #24, "Having a career outside the home is more valuable and fulfilling than being 'just' a wife and mom" in *LYWB* (pages 169–73).

REALIZE

1. Look up Proverbs 31:10–31. What responsibilities does the woman in this chapter have? List them below.

❖ _____

❖ _____

❖ _____

❖ _____

❖ _____

❖ _____

❖ _____

❖ _____

❖ _____

❖ _____

❖ _____

❖ _____

❖ _____

❖ _____

❖ _____

❖ _____

❖ _____

❖ _____

❖ _____

2. Go back through the list you made on the previous page. Write down some ideas for what these items look like in the life of a modern woman.

3. The Proverbs 31 woman is certainly capable of doing lots of good things with her life. But look closely at these verses. How would you summarize the focus of her efforts and priorities? What clues does this passage give you about what motivates her and enables her to joyfully embrace those priorities?

_____

_____

The woman in this passage has interests outside her home, but the primary focus of her daily activities is on serving her family and meeting their needs. She does not consider this a burden—her virtuous ("excellent") heart and her lifelong commitment to her husband and family flow out of her reverence for God (v. 30—she "fears the LORD").

4. Think back to the conversation with Rob and Ryan highlighted in this section. Ryan mentions that girls his age feel pressure not to be a wife and a mother. What advice would you offer to a friend who was feeling this kind of pressure? Use the verses you just read to back up your counsel.

_____

_____

_____

_____

5. What are some practical ways a young, single woman can apply the principles of Proverbs 31 to her life? (By the way, if you want to be a godly wife and mother someday, now is the time to start developing these characteristics!)

_____

_____

_____

_____

_____

_____

R RESPOND

1. What core messages do you think modern young women are receiving from our culture about marriage and motherhood? Here are some prompts to get you started.

❖ "It's okay to be a wife and mother, but _____ is more important."

❖ "You should accomplish _____ before becoming a wife and a mother."

❖ "Focusing on just becoming a wife and a mother is old-fashioned because _____ _____."

❖ "A woman who is just a wife and a mom is _____."

_____

_____

_____

2. The Proverbs 31 woman does have meaningful work outside her home, but she doesn't neglect the well-being of her husband and children. Why do you think being a wife and mother is such a worthwhile calling?

_____

_____

_____

3. In what ways has God uniquely gifted women so they can effectively serve as wives and mothers? How can they glorify God in those roles?

_____

_____

_____

_____

_____

_____

_____

4. Ask your mom or another mom you respect which roles give her the most fulfillment. Specifically, ask her if she is able to find meaning in her roles as a mother. Why does she think these roles are important?

_____

_____

_____

_____

_____

_____

PRAY ABOUT IT

Father, thank You for designing me with purpose. I realize that women are uniquely designed to . . .

_____

_____

_____

_____

_____

_____

_____

_____

_____

_____

_____

What I Do Now Doesn't Affect the Future

R READ

Read Lie #25, "What I do now doesn't affect the future," in *LYWB* (pages 173–75).

R REALIZE

1. Look up Galatians 6:7. Write the verse in your own words below.

---

2. According to this verse, every action and choice we make has consequences. What are the results of failing to recognize that?

---

3. Think back to the story in *LYWB* about the young celebrity who was photographed drunk. What consequences will she likely face as a result of her actions? List three.

---

4. The Bible makes clear that we will face consequences for our actions. Can you find an example in Scripture where a sinful choice led to specific consequences? Write the example below.

 RESPOND

1. Can you think of an example from your own life where a foolish choice led to painful consequences? Write about that experience below.

_____

_____

_____

_____

_____

_____

_____

_____

_____

_____

_____

2. Can you think of an example from your own life where a godly choice resulted in blessing? Write about that experience below.

_____

_____

_____

_____

_____

_____

_____

_____

_____

_____

_____

[lies young women believe]

3. Think back to middle school. If you could go back, what would you do differently?
Armed with that knowledge, make some decisions about what you can change now in order to positively impact your future.

----

4. No single choice will have a greater impact on your life than the choice to pursue a relationship with Christ. A key element of this pursuit is developing a regular habit of spending time in God's Word. We want to encourage you to take the thirty-day challenge presented on page 175 of this chapter in *LYWB*. Commit to spend time with the Lord in His Word every day for the next thirty days. Sign the pledge card, then hop on our blog at LiesYoungWomenBelieve.com and tell us about it, so we can cheer you on!

5. Decisions you make today could lead to Jesus being glorified through your life for years (or even generations) to come! How can you honor and serve Him in this season of your life? Here are some suggestions to get you started. Add others that the Lord may put on your heart. Put a check mark next to any steps you believe He is leading you to take.

_____ ❖ become more involved in your local church

_____ ❖ start a *Lies Young Women Believe* Bible study

_____ ❖ share the gospel with a non-Christian friend

_____ ❖ commit to standards for purity in your relationships with guys

_____ ❖ go on a short-term mission trip

_____ ❖ encourage a lonely person in your church or community

_____ ❖ _____

_____ ❖ _____

_____ ❖ _____

PRAY ABOUT IT

Lord, help me realize how my current choices will affect my future. Guide me toward the choices that most glorify You and direct me toward Your will for my life. I realize that I need to form new habits in the area of . . .

[lies young women believe]

A **ACT** **Plan a dinner date with a couple from your church.** Many of the girls we talked to said they didn't have any positive examples of happy marriages. This made it difficult for them to imagine that marriage might be a key part of God's plan for them. Make a dinner date with a happily married couple from your church. Ask how they met, how he proposed, and about the keys that have helped them develop a strong marriage. Who doesn't love to hear a real-life love story? You will likely learn that their marriage hasn't been perfect. Even so, we hope they will share with you that it has been one of the most important and fulfilling relationships they have.

A Collision with Truth

This week, you'll read chapters 13–15 in _LYWB_ (pages 179–202).

Catching a Glimpse

"Throughout this book, we've tried to expose the Deceiver and some of the lies you may have fallen for. That's an important part of overcoming lies. But we have an even more important goal, which brings us to the second key fact upon which this book was built. We want you to know that, no matter how trapped in your bondage you may feel: The truth has the power to set us free.

"Freedom! That's what we want for you. We're not talking about being free to do anything you want to do. True freedom is the power to do what God wants you to do; it is being free from the control of sinful ways of thinking, sinful attitudes, and sinful behavior patterns. It's knowing that, by God's grace, you can say no to sin and yes to God. Instead of being in bondage to the consequences of believing lies, you can be free."

(_Lies Young Women Believe,_ page 180–81)

KNOW
the
TRUTH

Here's the verse we'd like you to memorize this week:

"Jesus said to the Jews who had believed him, 'If you abide in my word, you are truly my disciples, and you will know the truth, and the truth will set you free'"

(JOHN 8:31–32)

DAY ONE:
Fighting the Lies

R READ
Read chapter 13 in *LYWB* (pages 179–85).

R REALIZE

1. Go back and look up James 1:14–15 (we first tackled this Scripture in chapter 2 of *LYWB*). Write out the Scripture below.

_____

_____

_____

_____

_____

_____

2. This passage describes the pattern of how temptation works in our lives. Write out the progression below. We've given you some prompts to help get your thinking rolling.

✦ Often, I am tempted to sin as a result of my desire for _____

_____

✦ That desire becomes sinful when I act on it by _____

_____

✦ The consequences of this sin are _____

_____

3. We can read about a time when Jesus was tempted in the book of Luke. The Deceiver acted on the pattern we just explored above by preying on natural, human desires, but Jesus did not sin. Look up this story in Luke 4:1–13 and use it to answer the following questions.

What specific desires did Satan promise to meet when he tempted Jesus?

_____

_____

[lies young women believe]

Jesus did more than just tell Satan no. What pattern do you see in the way He responded each time He was tempted?

_____

_____

Jesus refused to give in to His desires. He countered Satan's lies with Truth from the Word and He did not sin. We can find freedom from the bondage of lies by applying this same strategy.

R RESPOND

1. Think back to Nancy's story about the fruit flies. How has believing lies led to feeling trapped in your own life?

_____

_____

_____

_____

2. We hope this study has given you a new perspective on the power lies have to impact your life. What has helped the most?

_____

_____

_____

3. What has this study taught you about the power lies have to impact your life?

_____

_____

_____

_____

4. All of us have areas of our lives where we still need more of God's freedom. Let's walk through the steps outlined on pages 184–85 of *LYWB* to help you achieve freedom in one area. We've given you some examples to help you get started:

A. What is one area of bondage or sinful behavior you can identify in your life? For example: flirting

I am still feeling bondage in the area of:_ _

_ _

Every area of bondage or sinful behavior in our lives is rooted in a lie—something we've believed that is not true, according to God's Word. What lie might be at the root of the area of bondage you recorded above? If the answer is not immediately obvious, ask the Lord to show you what lie you believe. If you need help, turn to the table of contents in *LYWB* and look through the lies we've addressed. Identify one or more of those lies that you realize you believe. You may want to ask a spiritually mature friend or a mentor to help you see the lie that is influencing your behavior. For example: "I need a boyfriend."

One lie that I believe is at the root of this area of bondage in my life is: _ _ _ _ _ _ _ _ _

_ _

B. List any ways in which you have fueled that lie by listening to or dwelling on it.

_ _

_ _

_ _

_ _

C. What do you need to do to avoid listening to and dwelling on that lie from now on?

_ _

_ _

_ _

_ _

>> GREAT! HOLD THOSE THOUGHTS. We'll come back to this lie and how you can overcome it tomorrow!

[lies young women believe]

 PRAY ABOUT IT

Jesus, please give me the courage to take these actions. I especially need to know Your Truth in the area of . . . so I can walk in freedom.

Replacing the Lies with Truth

R READ

Read chapter 14 in *LYWB* (pages 187–92).

R REALIZE

1. Read John 14:6. Write it in your own words below.

_____

_____

_____

2. According to this verse, what is *the* source of Truth?

_____

3. Think back to Nancy's story in *LYWB* about being hurt by one of her coworkers. What was the result of her decision to replace the lies she had believed with the Truth she found in God's Word?

_____

_____

4. What consequences might she have experienced if she had made a different decision by choosing to dwell on lies instead of embracing Truth?

_____

_____

Nancy had a choice to either continue to believe lies or to embrace the Truth she found in God's Word. We have the same choice to make as we work through the process of identifying lies in our own lives. How we respond to God's Truth will ultimately determine our ability to be freed from the bondage of lies.

 # RESPOND

1. OK, now look back at what you recorded in the last lesson. Let's review.

❧ My area of bondage is: _____

_____

_____

❧ The lie (or lies) I believe is (are): _____

_____

_____

❧ I dwell on this lie by: _____

_____

_____

❧ I have determined to stop dwelling on it by: _____

_____

_____

In this lesson, we want to take it one step further.

2. What is the final—and most important—step in combating lies in our lives?

_____

_____

_____

Focusing on the *lies* was never the intent of this book. It is the *Truth* that will set you free! The final and most important step to combat lies is to focus on the Truth!

3. Take some extended time today to search through Scripture for the Truth that will set you free from your lie or lies. Use your Bible concordance to look up key words or go to BibleGateway.com to search for key words. You can also thumb through the verses found on pages 195–201 in *LYWB*. Compile a list of at least five verses and write them on the next page.

4. Cut this list out and put it in a place where you can see it and dwell on these truths each day. You might put it in your locker, on your bathroom mirror or in your Bible.

PRAY ABOUT IT

Jesus, thank You for being the Truth. Help me learn more about You through Your Word, and apply Your Truth to my life. I am learning to replace the lies in my life with the Truth that . . .

THE TRUTH WILL SET ME FREE!

>>>

LiesYoungWomenBelieve.com

Powerful Truths to Counter Everyday Lies

R READ
Read chapter 15 in *LYWB* (pages 195–202).

R REALIZE

1. Fill in the blanks for the following verse.

❖ "So whoever _____ the _____ _____ to do and _____

to _____ _____, for him it is _____." (JAMES 4:17)

2. How does this verse apply to the process of identifying lies and replacing them with Truth?

_____

_____

_____

_____

3. This chapter was written to arm you with the specific Truth you need to combat lies in twenty-two key areas. But just reading the list isn't likely to cause a major shift in your heart and life. What steps can you take to *know* the Truth outlined in this chapter? List three.

_____

_____

_____

_____

_____

_____

_____

R RESPOND

1. As you go through the list of Truths in this chapter, circle the ones that most speak to where you are in your life right now.

2. Consider the areas of temptation or sin where your generation seems to struggle most. What Truth can you add to those found in this chapter to combat a lie that is at the core of that struggle? Find Scriptures to back up the Truth.

_____

_____

_____

_____

3. If you haven't already done so, post this list somewhere you can review it often. We recommend placing it on your nightstand, in your locker, or on your bathroom mirror.

P PRAY ABOUT IT

Jesus, help me distinguish between Truth and lies. Thank You for using this study to free me from bondage in the area of . . .

_____

_____

_____

_____

_____

_____

_____

_____

DAY FOUR:
Becoming a Truth Speaker

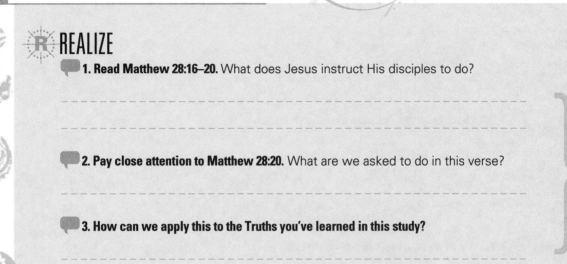

R REALIZE

1. Read Matthew 28:16–20. What does Jesus instruct His disciples to do?

----

2. Pay close attention to Matthew 28:20. What are we asked to do in this verse?

----

3. How can we apply this to the Truths you've learned in this study?

Jesus' words in this passage are often called the "Great Commission." Jesus encourages His disciples to go out and tell others about the good news of His death and resurrection. But He also asks them to teach others about all that He has commanded. You've learned a lot about God's commands and His Truth over the course of this study. Now it's time to tell others what you've learned about the power of Truth.

4. Look up 1 Timothy 4:12. Write that verse in your own words below.

----

5. According to this verse, when is the right time for you to model the power of Truth to others?

You don't have to wait until you are older to be an example to those around you. Now is the time! You can be a Truth-speaker starting today!

R RESPOND

1. List three lies that you have seen produce obvious consequences in the lives of your friends.

_____

_____

_____

2. Who have been the Truth speakers in your life?

_____

_____

_____

3. What was it about their approach that was effective?

_____

_____

_____

4. How can you approach others in this same way?

_____

_____

5. Think of a friend who is in bondage in some area of her life. What lie(s) do you think she may have believed? What Truth(s) could help set her free? Ask God to show you how and when to share your heart with her and to prepare her heart to receive the Truth.

_____

_____

_____

6. Make copies of the twenty-two Truths presented in chapter 15 to share with your friends. Commit to lovingly remind each other of specific Truths that apply to real-life situations you face.

[lies young women believe]

💗 PRAY ABOUT IT

Jesus, give me the courage to be a Truth-speaker to my generation. So many of my friends are believing lies like . . .

START A LIES YOUNG WOMEN BELIEVE BIBLE STUDY

Use the discussion questions in this guide to lead others through this material. You can find other great resources to help you get started on our website, **LiesYoungWomenBelieve.com.**

▶ ACT **Make a Truth bracelet.** If you're like us, you will need to be reminded to pursue Truth. Make a bracelet designed to remind you to continually seek God's Truth from His Word. It can be as simple as a piece of string or as elaborate as a bracelet with charms that remind you of specific Truths. Whenever you look at your bracelet, remember the lies you've been delivered from and the importance of regularly renewing your mind with the Truth of God's Word.

Ideas For Group Study

We strongly encourage you to go through this study with a group of other girls. To make discussion easy and fun, we have highlighted questions throughout the guide using this conversation symbol 💬. You can simply do the lessons, meet once a week, and look for the 💬 to get your conversations started!

Here are a few more ideas for how to start a group using this study.

1. Pray!

✤ If lives are changed as a result of this study it will be because of the power of God's Truth, and it will happen through the ministry and work of the Holy Spirit. It is important to stop and pray before you take action. Ask for God's guidance every step of the way. Pray for wisdom as you lead others through the material found in the book.

Ask others to pray with you. There are likely some women in your church or youth group who would love to help in this way. Ask women to pray for you, for other leaders, and for the girls who will be participating in the study.

2. Recruit!

✤ If you are a young woman desiring to lead this study with a group of your peers, recruit an older woman to help. Talk to your youth pastor's wife, your Sunday school teacher, your mom, or another adult woman you trust. They might be willing to open their home, provide snacks, or serve as a coleader.

The topics presented in this book may raise questions and issues that require maturity and discernment to handle. You may uncover areas of sin and hurt in the lives of the girls who are participating that you are unprepared to deal with on your own. Don't hesitate to ask for help from others. Your pastor and youth pastor are likely great resources. You can also check our blog to get advice and support from others.

3. Find a great location.

✤ It's easier to open up in an environment that feels warm and inviting. Be intentional about finding a meeting place that is comfortable and welcoming. Consider providing snacks or a meal. Food can help create a homey atmosphere.

4. Send out invitations.

❧ Send out paper invitations to the girls you would like to have in attendance. Be sure to include the time, date, and place of the study. You can also send out an event invitation through social media. Then, consider sending out weekly reminders through email or text.

Encourage the girls who attend to invite their friends—even those friends who aren't yet Christians. If each girl you invite invites just one other person, that will help get the word out to girls beyond your immediate circle of friends.

5. Set a reasonable pace.

❧ It is important that you don't try to cover too much ground too quickly; that's why this guide divides the material from *Lies Young Women Believe* into nine manageable weeks. Each chapter of this book is packed with Truth. If you try to race through it, you might miss something important.

6. Feel free to throw out the schedule.

❧ Even though we recommend planning out a schedule in advance, we also want you to have the freedom to abandon it at any point. There may be times when you need to veer from the outline and let the conversation take a different course. There may be occasions where you need to stop everything and simply love on a girl from your group who has opened up about some sin or hurt in her life. The impact of lies can be messy. Be sensitive to the leading of His Spirit and trust the Lord to help you know how to respond to situations that may arise in the course of discussion.

7. Make sure each girl has a copy of *Lies Young Women Believe* as well as a copy of this *Lies Young Women Believe Study Guide*.

❧ Much of the information in this book needs to be processed at an individual level. Girls will need time to think through the information and process it on their own. If each girl has her own books, she can read through the main book and journal in the Bible study between meeting times.

8. Use our website as a resource.

❧ You can share this experience with other girls who are pursuing Truth. Tap into what God is doing in others' lives. Hop on to **LiesYoungWomenBelieve.com** any time you have a question or prayer need or want to share how you are being set free by the Truth that is in Christ! You can also follow us on Instagram: **@LiesYoungWomenBelieve** and on Twitter: **@LYWBblog**.

Offering sound, biblical teaching and encouragement for women through . . .

Books & Resources Nancy's books, True Woman Books, and a wide range of audio/video

Broadcasting Two daily, nationally syndicated broadcasts (*Revive Our Hearts* and *Seeking Him*) reaching over one million listeners a week

Events & Training True Woman Conferences and events designed to equip women's ministry leaders and pastors' wives

Internet ReviveOurHearts.com, TrueWoman.com, and LiesYoungWomenBelieve.com; daily blogs, and a large, searchable collection of electronic resources for women in every season of life

Believing God for a grassroots movement of authentic revival and biblical womanhood . . .

Encouraging women to:

- Discover and embrace God's design and mission for their lives.
- Reflect the beauty and heart of Jesus Christ to their world.
- Intentionally pass on the baton of truth to the next generation.
- Pray earnestly for an outpouring of God's Spirit in their families, churches, nation, and world.

The truth may not change your circumstances, but it will change you.

THE TRUTH WILL SET YOU FREE

Go online for more
lie-breaking resources

Explore more books helping readers counter
lies with the Truth, please visit

LIESBOOKS.COM

The Power of Modesty for Tweens!

MOODY
Publishers®

From the Word to Life®

True Girl is geared to helping tween girls understand their dignity in Christ. It features a creative self-help text format that includes sidebars, quizzes, games, exploded quotes, and graphics to help them absorb the message. This book pairs with *True Girl Mom-Daughter Devos*, providing moms a helpful resource for walking their tween girl through this formative time. | **MyTrueGirl.com**

TRUE GIRL 978-0-8024-1971-2

MOM/DAUGHTER DEVOS 978-0-8024-1972-9 | ALSO AVAILABLE AS EBOOKS

Abstinence isn't about **not** having sex— it's about waiting to have it **right**.

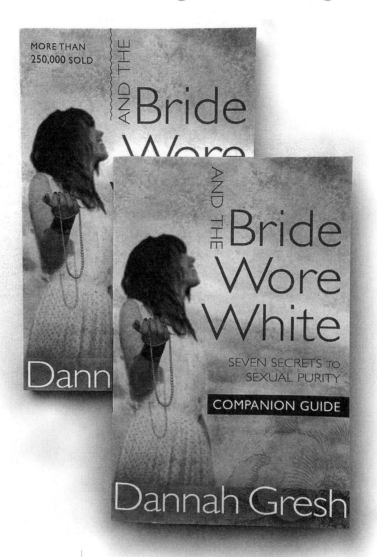

BIBLE VERSES

Each week you'll have a memory challenge.
Just pull out the card for that week,
and start reviewing until the Scripture
is stored deep down in your heart.

{ WEEK 1 }

"So flee youthful passions and pursue righteousness, faith, love, and peace, along with those who call on the Lord from a pure heart."

(2 TIMOTHY 2:22)

{ WEEK 2 }

"Are not five sparrows sold for two pennies? And not one of them is forgotten before God. Why, even the hairs of your head are all numbered. Fear not; you are of more value than many sparrows."

(LUKE 12:6–7)

{ WEEK 3 }

"Finally, be strong in the Lord and in the strength of his might. Put on the whole armor of God, that you may be able to stand against the schemes of the devil. For we do not wrestle against flesh and blood, but against the rulers, against the authorities, against the cosmic powers over this present darkness, against the spiritual forces of evil in the heavenly places."

(EPHESIANS 6:10–12)

{ WEEK 4 }

"But among you there must not be even a hint of sexual immorality, or of any kind of impurity, or of greed, because these are improper for God's holy people."

(EPHESIANS 5:3 NIV)

{ WEEK 5 }

"Greater love has no one than this, that someone lay down his life for his friends. You are my friends if you do what I command you. No longer do I call you servants, for the servant does not know what his master is doing; but I have called you friends, for all that I have heard from my Father I have made known to you."

(JOHN 15:13–15)

{ WEEK 6 }

"If you confess with your mouth that Jesus is Lord and believe in your heart that God raised him from the dead, you will be saved. For with the heart one believes and is justified, and with the mouth one confesses and is saved."

(ROMANS 10:9–10)